SHARE YOUR
MESSAGE
WITH THE
WORLD

TONY GAMBONE

BALBOA.
PRESS
A DIVISION OF HAY HOUSE

Balboa Press books may be ordered through booksellers or by contacting:

Balboa Press
A Division of Hay House
1663 Liberty Drive
Bloomington, IN 47403
www.balboapress.com
1 (877) 407-4847

Print information available on the last page.

ISBN: 978-1-5043-4863-8 (sc)
ISBN: 978-1-5043-4865-2 (hc)
ISBN: 978-1-5043-4864-5 (e)

Library of Congress Control Number: 2016900582

Balboa Press rev. date: 01/18/2016

Foreword

Welcome to a new adventure. In Volume I of *Share Your Message with the World* you heard inspirational stories of struggle and accomplishment. We hope you found those stories encouraging and helpful to your personal journey.

Through the stories in Volume II, you will discover proven ways to rise above things that have held you back. You will learn from amazing individuals who by empowering their own lives went on to not only create a beautiful life but to also help others find their life's purposes. These authors have come together to share with you life strategies that take you from where you are to where you want to be.

You will learn ways to discover your passion and live the life you have always dreamed. Many of these stories will motivate you to leave the fear and destructive life patterns behind and become the leader of your own life.

My friend, Tony Gambone, applied his positive attitude and commitment to excellence to create this project because he knows the importance of sharing your message and how it can change the lives of many. May this book open doors and stimulate curiosity that will catapult you into a new life.

Linda Ballesteros, Author, Radio Host
Co-Founder of MPower Learning Connection

Thank You

As always I first give Thanks to God for all the Blessings that have taken place for me through this journey. I must thank all of the authors that were willing to share their messages in this book with everyone.

Big Thanks to my wife, Wendy Gambone, for supporting me with every step of the book and the time that she gave to helping put this book together. And thank you Linda Ballesteros for taking the time to write the forward in this book. Finally, thanks to all of you who have chosen to read these stories, may they encourage and inspire you.

Introduction

I have been interviewing people for over 40 years. Becoming a Radio Host was something that lead me to fully understand the power of listening.

When I decided to do a compilation book for others to tell the story of their journey in life I did not realize that it would turn out the way it did. I thought that if I could get people to tell a story about how they overcame the everyday challenges in their life it would empower other to do the same.

It turned out that it did empower others as they read the different stories told by the authors in *Share Your Message with The World Vol. I*. But what I did not recognized was how it would empower the authors and myself. I have learned that when we write down what has happened in life over the years we become empowered. It helps us realize all the great things that have happened in our lives along the way.

Most of the time we get stuck on all the things that have gone wrong instead of focusing on all the things that went right. Living in a very busy and noisy world, we sometimes forget the good things along the way. I often say that telling your personal journey will make any bumpy road seem like it just had a few speed bumps in it.

After the first volume of *Share Your Message with The World* was released people started reaching out and asking if we were going to do a volume two. After much thought I decided to move forward on starting the second volume and get more people to Share Their Message.

I hope that by reading the stories in this book you will be empowered to tell someone your story. Most of the time, if we can just look back and see our journey it will empower us to move forward with a better mindset.

Alison Gentry

Alison Gentry is a wife, a mother, a working professional, a daughter, a friend, and a child of the one true King. After living on every coast of the United States and some points in between, Alison now calls the great state of Texas home. She received her MA in Human Services with an emphasis in Marriage and Family from Liberty University and is currently working on her MA in Professional Counseling in order to obtain her licensure in Professional Counseling from the state of Texas. At present, Alison serves as Director of the Houston campus for Belhaven University as well as an adjunct instructor in social services and psychology.

Learn more about Alison:

Website: www.vivifyministries.org
Email: alison.gentry@outlook.com
Social Media Links:
Facebook: facebook.com/saralis77
LinkedIn: linkedin.com/pub/alison-gentry-ma/30/910/753

Chapter 1

YOU MAKE ME BRAVE!

By Alison Gentry

When I was little I recall being so angry at the world and everyone in it. I was always desperate for attention, but always seemed to experience rejection instead. I was three when my parents brought my brother home from the hospital. That's when the anger really began to manifest. Up to that point, I had been the center of my parent's world. I hated my brother, because I felt I had been replaced.

I was always strong willed. I hated to go to bed. My parents were so desperate some nights to get me to go to sleep that they created the goodnight fairy to bring me wrapped treats after I was asleep. The first day of kindergarten, Mom drove me to school and I decided right away that I did not like the teacher and I wasn't going in the classroom. Mom took me aside and told me that I had two options, I could go in, or could go home and get a spanking. I chose the spanking. To me, spankings did not hurt. As my parents spanked me, I would just tell myself in my mind that it did not hurt. I knew that pain was psychological.

We moved a lot, I never fully settled anywhere. I went to new schools almost every year. School was boring for me. I would master the lesson and sit and wait on the other kids to finish. That's when I always managed to find trouble. I remember going to parent-teacher conferences with Mom and Dad. Different teachers at different times would tell my parents the same thing, "Alison is so smart; she's just too disruptive."

I ended up failing fifth grade when my parents divorced. When my parents told me that they were divorcing, I honestly thought, "Good! Now I only have to deal with one of you!" Dad transferred, and Mom stayed in California with my brother and me. I was constantly getting into trouble in school. Mom was now a single mother trying to go to college while working and was continually being called away to come address my behavioral issues. One day walking home from school, a group of girls jumped me and beat me to a pulp! I had no idea who these girls were or why they decided to target me. And, where I had been angry before, I was now raging. I decided to trust no one, and I intended never to trust anyone again. My motto was "I am going to screw you before you screw me." I began running away from home and fighting in school, finally getting expelled. Mom had finally had enough. She sent me to live with my dad who had moved to Louisiana.

Dad worked a lot, so I was left home alone often, a teenager's dream right? I experienced a lot of culture shock going from California to New Orleans, and I attended another new school. Because of my prior inattention to schoolwork and expulsion from school, I was far behind my peers. Unable to catch up, I experienced my second scholastic failure, the seventh grade. I had managed to make some friends, though. They invited me over one weekend while their parents were out of town. It was here that I experienced another blow to my humanity; I was raped by one of the guys from my school. He also humiliated me by spreading inappropriate and untrue gossip when we returned to school. I eventually managed to get expelled for fighting and running away from school. I put Dad through hell that year. I had a party at his house when he was out of town and my "friends" stole his jewelry and destroyed his house when a fight broke resulting in holes in the wall and blood on the carpet. Another time when he was out of town, I stole my grandmother's car. I had never driven before and managed to demolish the neighbor's mailbox and drive through Dad's kitchen wall. Afraid, I ran away. I ran away numerous times after that, overdosed on meds, became extremely promiscuous and just did not care if I died or hurt anyone in the process.

I was admitted to a mental health facility for behavioral disorders. For my first escape, I was able to jump the fence and make it a few miles before the police caught me. My second attempt involved friends who helped by setting fire on the outside of the Plexiglas window to melt it. We were succeeding until a nurse caught me and placed me in solitary confinement for three days. I was left with nothing except a mattress, my grandfather's Bible, and me. I treasured that Bible and loved seeing his handwritten notes. The Holy Spirit met me there and planted seeds, but it would be several years before I surrendered.

I was diagnosed as bipolar and sent home with a truckload of lithium. Dad couldn't handle me any longer and called Mom with an ultimatum – "Take her back or she becomes a ward of the state." Mom moved me back to California. She couldn't handle me alone so we moved to her home state of Mississippi. Family told her they would offer support in raising me, but when they saw how difficult I was, all support disappeared any time I was around.

It didn't take long for me to find the "wrong crowd" and continue my desperate and despicable behavior. When I was fourteen, friends and I stole a car to runaway to Houston, TX. I handled the driving really well until the police pulled us over. We landed in Juvenile hall.

After this incident Mom sought help through the local mental health facility where I was eventually transferred to another hospital for long term treatment. I learned about human behavior in these facilities. I acted crazy at times, but here I came face-to-face with authentic crazy. I was smart. I would master the facilities program, the staff would fall in love with me and I would quickly excel.

Before I finally called it quits, Mom enrolled me in a private Christian school where I failed ninth grade. That was it for me. I dropped out, and no one could make me go. I refused. Numerous outbursts followed before I was committed to the state mental facility. I hated my parents. They were both tired – tired of trying, tired of fighting for me and with me, tired of losing – just tired. During one of our last family counseling sessions, Dad refused to parent me and Mom asked that I be made a ward of the state. I was sixteen. My doctor made the arrangements and called parents to sign the paperwork. The doctor explained to my parents that once a ward of the state, they would not be allowed any contact with me until my twenty-first birthday, and only if I chose to have contact with them. Dad was ready to sign, but Mom just couldn't do it. Although she strongly disliked me at the time for all the hell I had put her through, she loved me more and could not bear the thought of not seeing me or talking to me for five years and possibly the rest of her life. She stopped the proceedings.

I went home with her where she pretty much left me alone and let me do what I wanted to do. I became involved in an unhealthy relationship and got pregnant. Mom made it clear that she would not raise my child and suggested I place the baby for adoption. Mom took me to a mission-based pregnancy center where I met with a lady who helped me realistically understand everything involved in caring for a child. Although I wanted my child desperately, I knew it was best that I place him for adoption. Again a huge piece of me died the day I placed him.

Nine months after placing my child I found myself pregnant again, but this time there was no way I was doing it again. I was eighteen and determined to do whatever it took to parent my child. While the father was identical to my previous child's father and began to cheat on me, I decided that I could do it without him. Single parenting was perhaps harder than placing in some respects. It required me to die to self, and I was not ready. I left my daughter frequently with Mom and went partying. I ended up getting pregnant one more time and decided that there was no way that I could place or parent. On Good Friday of 1998, I found myself somewhere I never thought I would be, an abortion clinic. I sat there and begged God to forgive me. This act thrust me into the abyss. I felt there was no hope for me. Mom kept asking me what was wrong, but I was so ashamed that I could not tell anyone, until one night I decided to tell her. She proceeded to tell me the story of King David and how he had murdered Bathsheba's husband, but was still considered a man after God's own heart. I felt a glimmer of hope.

While I still was not ready to give up the party life completely at twenty-one, I slowed down a bit. One night I was on my way to the club and I heard in a small, still voice, "Alison, go home and get on your knees." I knew that I was in the presence of the Lord. The enemy was there too. He said, "Alison, you go home and get on your knees..." and started naming all the things that my fleshed loved. I was a marijuana dealer at the time – good, easy money. I had a boyfriend who was terrible for me. I enjoyed all things with no eternal value. Jesus said to me, "But Alison, with me you will have eternal life." I chose to go home and get on my knees. I prayed and the Holy Spirit came upon me as I surrendered that night. I realized my desperate need for a Savior. I immediately wanted to purge myself of all things unclean, movies, music, friends, you name it. It was difficult, and it was scary.

Because of my obedience, the Lord began to bless me quickly. I got a great job, received a promotion in less than a year and transferred to Jacksonville, Florida where I got involved in a phenomenal church, a single mom's bible study, and leading a youth group. After a year, I felt like God was calling me into missions. I sold everything I owned, packed up and joined Youth with a Mission. My daughter and I got to travel and see things in other countries we otherwise would have never seen.

Having already obtained my GED, I started college. I received a Bachelor's and Master's, and now I am working on my Licensure in Counseling. Who would have ever thought after all this rebellion, tragedy, and heartache that God would be using me to accomplish His Kingdom work? He gave me courage. He made me brave. He called me; I answered. He said go, I went, and still am just like King David. God used him to defeat Goliath. He uses the unlikely; He empowers; He redeems. He made me brave enough to leave all the hurt, all the rejection, all the disappointment behind. For to me, to live as Christ and to die is gain. My life verse has become Romans 8:18 "I consider that sufferings of this present time are not worth comparing with the glory that will be revealed in us." There is no situation that is too desperate, no person who has done too much or is too far gone that God is not able to redeem and restore to a life worth living. Can you hear Him calling? Be brave!

Allison Schaberg

Allison Schaberg has spent more than 20 years in the insurance and financial services industry. Owner and Managing Partner of Consolidated Planning Group, she operates an agency in Sugar Land, TX which serves a multi-state area. Allison and her team are focused on helping their clients reach their financial goals and objectives through comprehensive planning afforded by both insurance products and investment vehicles.

Allison started in the business at a very young age. In fact, she says that she accidently got into the business but on purpose she stayed when the business got into her! She has a passion and a heart for serving others and an affinity to working with families that have unique and challenging needs.

She is married to her wonderful husband Jeff. They are members of River Point Church. They enjoy scuba diving and spending time with their four kids.

Learn more about Allison:
Website: www.consolidatedplanninggroup.com
Email: aschaberg.cpg@gmail.com
Social Media Links:
LinkedIn: linkedin.com/pub/allison-schaberg/76/334/b53

Chapter 2

LIFE IS A GIFT

Is your house in order?

By Allison Schaberg

Professionally my career has been dedicated to insurance and financial services. Personally, I wear many hats, wife, mother, daughter, sister, caregiver, homeschooler, educator, board member, small group leader, nurse, taxi driver, and the list goes on and on. Whether you call me Allison, mom, Mrs. Schaberg, friend, family, advisor, or co-worker all would agree that I am truly thankful for each of these roles.

As president of Consolidated Planning Group in Sugar Land, TX my team and I stand proud to be a premier provider of insurance and financial services serving both Texas and North Carolina. Through a holistic approach to planning we custom design strategies based on one's needs, wants, and goals for their future. I actually got started in the industry at 15 on a workers permit and have been in the business for over 20 years. I like to say that I accidently got into the business but when the business got into me, on purpose I stayed! I've been blessed to be in a career that truly feels philanthropic in the way that I am able to serve others.

For as long as I can remember professionally I have been sharing a clear and concise message about the importance of having one's financial house in order. In short, bad things typically happen to other people. From the chair that I sit in I hear many heart wrenching stories of failing to plan. In the past I did a lot of volunteer work with the Children's Miracle Network. This was long before my children came along. Nevertheless, I was always humbled by those families and their stories. I was equally humbled by the fact that despite their horrific circumstances, these families were thankful for each new day and celebrated things that most of us take for granted. Those kids had literally been through hell and back but somehow still managed to smile through it all. Through these interactions I was able to see the difference that planning made when the unthinkable happened. I learned at a very young age that vocationally, financial services was not only were I needed to be but where I wanted to be. To this day it gives me great satisfaction and pleasure to assist my clients by helping them reach their financial goals one step at a time.

Passionate about my work and determined to make smart financial decisions, I purchased my first Life insurance contract at the age of 19 and subsequently bought additional policies to include Disability and Long Term Care and even started a small systematic investment plan. Some people thought it was crazy since at that time I wasn't married, didn't have kids, and didn't own a home. I pressed on anyway because I knew in my heart of hearts that one day I would have all those things and would need protection. It just made so much sense to me to lock my age in while I was young and insurable. I profoundly believed in this and onward I marched!

Although I didn't know then, every season of my life was equipping me and preparing me for a future that at times others would call unbelievable, bad luck, or just plain sad. For me though, it was just my life and I wasn't upset or sad about it. People would say, "I don't know how you do what you do". My first thought always went back to one of my favorite quotes by an unknown author "when you change the way you look at things, what you look at changes". Then, I would simply reply, you just do.

You see at the age of 3 my daughter was diagnosed with Leukemia. She went from being a completely healthy little girl to critically sick, on life support, with a very questionable future. She had a mass in her chest that had collapsed one of her lungs and partially collapsed the other. Due to the size of the mass we didn't know if we would ever get the chance to fight the Leukemia. At that moment my life seemed to be flashing before my eyes and changed in an instant. Clearly you have a renewed sense of appreciation for the things that are important in life and the things that just aren't. Funny how that was the exact same humbling feeling I had all those years ago with my volunteerism through CMN. Even in the midst of her illness I have to say that I felt like the lucky one. I felt lucky because her treatment facility was less than an hour away. We had family support in the area and we had hope that many of the families did not. Many families lost their jobs, their insurance, their marriage and in the end their child too. Yep, we were lucky!

I didn't know that my volunteer work with the Children's Miracle network was preparing me for my own child to have Leukemia and three years of chemotherapy while I was expecting my second child. I didn't know that it was preparing me for two special needs kids. I didn't know that I would have pregnancy complications and be put on disability during that pregnancy. After all, I had always been healthy. Really for almost a ten year period it was one blow after another. So much so, that it would make for a really interesting made for TV movie one day!

Just when I could finally see light at the end of the tunnel things would take another last minute turn. I was referred to a new client from one of my dearest existing clients. When I met her for the first time she shared her journey and story of Breast Cancer. I was able to help her make some good decisions about the insurance she already had in place. I explained the importance of never letting it go. After a few days had passed she called me one afternoon to just say thank you for helping her. After hearing her story there was a small voice in my head prompting me to go get a mammogram. Younger than the age recommended for mammograms, without symptoms, lumps, bumps, or family history I was diagnosed with Breast Cancer!

To say that I was absolutely shocked would be an extreme understatement! In fact I was so convinced that they were wrong I actually had my biopsies sent to three different pathologists at three different facilities to be read. Well, as much as I hoped I was right, I was not. All three facilities agreed on the diagnosis of Breast Cancer. Soon we would find out that I had an unfortunate gene that is linked to young diagnoses of breast cancer and can also be linked to pediatric leukemia's. I had no choice but to have a bi-lateral mastectomy and reconstruction. Vocationally we help people plan ahead in case they live too long, die too soon, become disabled along the way. These types of things happen to other people, right? My life was flashing in front of me once again. At times it was so surreal that I would find myself thinking "is this really happening, I mean, really." I've often thought how ironic it was that, my client referral called me to say thank you. The word thank you seems so inadequate for what she did for me by sharing her story.

My story has a happy ending. My daughter is now 14 and moved from in remission to cured, from her Leukemia in 2011. We locked in her age at age one on life insurance that also has a guaranteed insurability option. Thankfully, this was prior to her diagnosis. Although now she is uninsurable for the rest of her life no one can ever take that coverage away from her. We had great health insurance, a cancer plan that paid for things that health insurance didn't, and I personally had a disability plan that paid me while I was unable to work through the pregnancy. After more than 2 million in medical bills through proper planning, insurance, and investments, those bills are paid.

As for the complicated pregnancy, a beautiful baby girl was born just two weeks early and was extremely healthy at 9lbs 2oz. Duke

Hospital was able to harvest and store her cord blood in case her sister would ever need a bone marrow transplant.

As for me I was lucky that I caught my breast cancer early. With what I had, had I waited until age 40 (3 more years) to get a mammogram as it is recommended I would have either been dead by then or had stage 4 metastatic cancer. I am uninsurable very likely for the rest of my life but luckily practice what I preach and already had my Life, Health, Disability, Cancer, and Long Term Care insurance in place for my family. One could have never convinced me before that I would be uninsurable at such a young age. I can't tell you how happy I am that I did the planning that I did, when I did it!

Because I followed my inner voice and got a mammogram I was able to dodge the bullet of chemotherapy and radiation. Despite the challenges that I have been faced with I have to say that I have been so blessed! Every step has been guided. It wasn't happenstance the work I did with CMN. It isn't happenstance that my profession is Insurance & Financial Services. Nor was it happenstance that I was transferred to Houston from North Carolina. It wasn't happenstance that my child was diagnosed with Leukemia or that I was diagnosed with Breast Cancer. It wasn't happenstance the people that have crossed my path both personally and professionally that led to important revelations.

Although sometimes I was left scratching my head wondering why things had happened the way they did, I have to say that God has truly had me right where he needed me to be each time and right on time! Truly there are reasons behind all of the seasons of our life. I wanted to be a nurse when I grew up. God had other plans for me. However, HE showed me through practice with my own child that nursing as a career certainly wasn't my passion! It's funny how things have a way of working out.

It's important for me to share that in spite of healthcare reform regardless of the recommendations one must trust their inner voice when it comes to their own health or their child's health. Specifically, go get that test, follow up, scan, or wellness check if you need it. Press on when something isn't right and ask questions. You know your body better than anyone else. Trust your own instinct. Your health may not fall into the nine dots of the masses. Additionally, many people put off insurance and planning for their future. It's not about beating yourself up about what you haven't done it's about taking the first step or in some cases taking the next step. Having your financial house in order is a process but it doesn't have to be painful nor is it as expensive as one might think. In the end, when the "IF's" in life happen to you and you hit a bump in the road, you will be prepared.

My heart is to spread awareness through my story. My hope is that it will inspire others to embrace the things that they've been putting off as it relates to their personal health and financial health. The small steps that one takes today may make all the difference in the world later. If by advocacy through sharing my story helps one other person have a happy ending as opposed to a catastrophic one I feel thankful for that opportunity.

Barbara Minton

Barbara Minton, is currently working as a Broker Associate with REALM Real Estate Professionals in Katy as she cultivates her desire to share the love and manifestations of Orbs. She lives in the Fort Bend County area with her husband and two sons. A college graduate from Central Michigan University, with a published book, "Orbs". She grew up in Michigan, riding horses, flying planes, sharing a loving and nurturing childhood from loving parents with her five sisters, six girls in seven years, all very close!

Learn more about Barbara:
Website: www.orbseeking.com
Email: barb@orbseeking.com
Phone: 713-417-0245
Social Media Links:

LinkedIn: linkedin.com/barbaraminton

Chapter 3

THE HEALING PROCESS OF LOSING A LOVED ONE

By Barbara Minton

Barbara had an experience with another Realm…another world living amongst us all the time. Her first book "Orbs" A Colorful Ethereal Experience; takes the reader on a journey that starts with the passing of her mother, October 7, 2010, then, through a series of odd "Coincidences" of a spiritual nature, that started to happen to her during the holiest week of the year for Christians, the week just before Easter and months after her mother's passing. She has a Bachelor of Fine Arts degree in photography, but found making money by taking photographs for others was not fulfilling. Before her mom passed, she stressed to her the importance of sharing her photographic gift with the world. Barbara believes she may have been the one who opened up the portal to this supernatural realm for her to become engaged within.

Her book contains a short story of how, where, when and why they started to come to her, it is a very colorful, overwhelming strength and a power that filled her with a new excitement for life. The interaction that started with the Orbs helped her immensely through the process and the depth of grief that she was going through. She shares pictures of Orbs dancing in the trees, teasing animals and dodging children. The fascinating world of Orbs is shared in full color photographs as the reader experiences the range and depth of the colors, and the intricate, spiritual, geometric designs within them as well as the playful way they communicate with us. This book can bring the reader a whole new level of insight as they feel the peace and connection to God, nature, animals and other humans through a universal bond shared by all.

Everyone goes through trials and tribulations in life, God is always here for us, he gives us guardian angels, signs and messages. The Orbs are another purpose that unifies us to God's power and presence always around us. So often we are wrapped up in all the "Stuff" in our lives, too busy to recognize the presence of these loving entities. Some people may scoff them off by saying that they are dust or water spots on the lens, but you will see proof in this book, that is incorrect. Her book invites you to explore a phenomenon by believing in the unseen, capturing the light, the love and the peace that surrounds us all. It is the author's personal journey of a spiritual transformation. She describes encounters and shares astounding, colorful photographs of her passage into what some might call an ethereal dimension currently around us.

On January 7th, 2015 her father left to join her mother in the next realm. Barbara shared a loving life with her parents along with her five sisters. Her parents had six girls in seven years, all very close who continue to keep their love and legacy alive by uniting their grandchildren together at least twice a year. The strength of family has always been so important for them! For her second book, Barbara has been compiling more photos of Orbs, but, with more pictures of them interacting with people and animals, which she plans on sharing with the world in 2016, look of it.

Through this book, "Share Your Message with the World II" you are given an opportunity to learn from others what life can offer by waking up, go outside the norm, communing with nature, following your intuition to take a chance and by sharing your gifts with others who can learn from you. Volunteer to unify your light and love with the world. Do not miss this chance to learn more about Orbs, as they are here for you, to connect YOU to the Divine. Seek, grow, learn, become.

Carolyn Sinclair

Carolyn Sinclair graduated UofH D with a Bachelor of Science in Applied Mathematics. She's been a business woman and entrepreneur. Although her background is analytical and scientific in nature, she easily bridges the gap between science and the esoteric.

For two decades Carolyn has studied and practiced with Asian masters. She's attended months of retreats and traveled to China three times. She's taught Tai Chi, qigong, walking and sitting meditation, given talks, seminars and been featured on Radio and TV. Thousands of hours of walking meditation has given her deep insight into the mysteries and benefits of this profound meditation.

Learn more about Carolyn:
Website: www.walking-meditation.com
Email: info@walking-meditation.com
Social Media Links:
Facebook: Facebook.com/Walking-Meditation-With-Carolyn

Chapter 4

WALKING MEDITATION

When Life Throws You a Curve Ball

By Carolyn Sinclair

I'm no saint, not a monk, nor have any desire to become one. I'm not a do-gooder, but try to do the right thing, and be sensitive to other people's feelings. I'm not antisocial; I like people and have no intention of living on a mountaintop. I love red wine, chocolate and sweets, but will exercise and blend up a green drink. At 65, a young spirit keeps me dancing to the rhythm of Salsa or West Coast Swing and uncontrollable belly laugher delights my soul. However, I also love the sound of my own silence and have meditated thousands of hours and participated in months of retreats. My philosophy is to be sincere with life but not overly serious. Am I a contradiction? Yes, like most everyone, I'm a living paradox. A gentle soul with a bit of a renegade spirit.

I was raised in an Irish Catholic family and considered an ordinary child. I was painfully shy and thought most of my eight other siblings smarter than I. In many ways I was invisible. At an early age my teachers dubbed me an under achiever, seemingly not having any particular outstanding skill or discernable quality. I didn't like homework, hated math, but thankfully managed to squeak by and finish high school with C's.

Now you might be thinking this was not a good start in life. But being somewhat invisible combined with a curious nature was a gift. I never had to live up to anyone else's expectations. It allowed me to fly under the radar, undetected to chart my unique path. It gave me a certain freedom.

When eighteen, I moved away from home. By nineteen I went on a six week Euro Rail pass around Europe. At twenty I moved to New York and became a flight attendant. By twenty five the man of my dreams showed up and we married. In my early thirties I completed a degree in Applied Mathematics.

I don't profess to have all the answers. Just when you think you do have life figured out, it throws you a curve ball, a wild pitch! In an instant, it hits you between the eyes. It's at those times we need something solid to rely on. Many derive inner strength through a strong spiritual foundation. I do too, but I see meditation as a necessary part of our inner journey to peace, health and joy.

In general, meditation is like a silent prayer. With practice it can unify our mind, body and spirit. It's our silent communion with Existence, The Infinite and our Creator. It can calm the mind, bringing a sense of balance and compassion as well as optimize health, reduce stress and maximize joy. It helps train our mind to live in the present moment and doesn't require any religious affiliation.

Although most are familiar with the concept of sitting meditation, most haven't heard of walking meditation. This ancient and profound form of meditation has largely gone unnoticed. Walking meditation is a dynamic meditation - meditation in motion. You don't remove yourself from the world. It helps bring peace into our daily lives, while being active. You can practice almost anywhere; down a hallway at work, in your living room or even a shopping mall. But outside in nature is the best! We walk every day. It doesn't cost a penny, no equipment is necessary, and it can easily be incorporated into your daily life.

Walking meditation has brought me through my darkest hours and continues to be part of my foundation for inner peace, happiness and wholeness. We cannot avoid life or a little rain on our parade. There are times when we all struggle with life circumstances. I'm no different. I'm not immune to life's challenges. But walking meditation has helped me heal faster, become more resilient and bring more balance and peace into my life. So how did a seemingly ordinary person, with a very conservative upbringing, find this beautiful, simple, yet profound form of meditation? This is where my story begins.

Aside from normal issues a couple might have after being married nearly twenty five years, we basically had a good relationship. My husband was my best friend, lover and companion. We actually *played* together – tennis, golf, jogging and enjoyed many similar interests. By all accounts people thought we had the ideal marriage. But wanting to improve, I decided that the little nagging issues confronting us could be resolved if only I could become more accepting and tolerant. So I enrolled in a Tai Chi course.

For one weekend a month, for several months, I took classes from a Chinese guru who visited Houston. At first I couldn't imagine why I decided to take Tai Chi. It was like practicing in slow motion. I was used to playing tennis, moving fast and *eating* the ball at the net! Am I really doing this? It really forced me to slow down, which was so unlike me. But in a strange way I enjoyed the peacefulness and practiced every day and could tell that it was making a difference.

One day while practicing under a tree my hand came near a leaf. Amazingly, I felt there was an energetic difference between the energy around the leaf and my hand flowing through the air. It felt as though I had put my hand in a liquid, like water, but it was just air, and of course not wet. Hmmm? Was I feeling energy around the leaf? Is there really such a thing? Was it my imagination?

Scientists understand that everything in the universe is energetic. Quantum physics confirms that even on an atomic level, we are energy. We say things like this person has good or bad energy. We also know how draining it can be when interacting with negative, complaining people. Right? So we all feel energy and are empathic to some degree. Food is converted into what? Energy! Air in our bodies is converted to what? Energy! Is it so impossible to think that if animals can recognize and feel energy that we can too? Do we think we are born inferior to animals? The mystics believe that everyone has the sensitivity to feel energy along with many other, seemingly, miraculous abilities. It's just that these abilities aren't activated and lay dormant.

Something had awakened in me for which I was totally unprepared. Suddenly I became sensitive to other people's emotions and illness. If I sat next to a person with kidney or heart problems my kidneys or heart would ache, and I would get fatigued. And forget about being around large groups of people! It was a nightmare and it was interfering with my life! I wanted my old life back!

Was this really happening to me? I'm not from California or Sedona, AZ. I have a normal husband, normal friends and a normal life. I came from a large, practical, hardworking family. No time for this kind of way-out silliness. I'm logical! I have a degree in mathematics damn it! Things like this don't happen to people like me. Yet I was experiencing a phenomena which I couldn't explain nor control.

I was changing, my life was changing and little did I know that my relationship with my husband was changing. I can't tell you exactly what he was thinking about my new ability, although he seemed to be understanding and taking it in stride. But can someone who has *not* experienced this super sensitivity to other people's emotions or illness for themselves, really understand? Especially when it happened so quickly. Although we were both basically good people, our relationship began to suffer.

As time went on I became more sensitive and our lack of communication grew and intimacy was lost. In the end, we both ended up changed by an event that neither had bargained for. I know it takes two to make or break a relationship. But fueled by his indifference a huge chasm began to form separating a couple that had once been deeply connected and best of friends. In addition, business related issues and an unexplainable, empathic, physical issue created further divide. Everything was beginning to crumble.

By the end of 1999 my husband had almost entirely stopped talking to me. When I would press him about what he was thinking he would just give me a cold, dark glare. Where had the good man I married gone? All I could feel was his disdain, anger and darkness piercing my heart. Being empathic only magnified the physical and emotional effects on me. His love was slipping away and my heart was broken. He couldn't understand my unique and newly acquired empathic abilities nor my related problems. He shut me out and I was devastated! In a blink of an eye he stopped loving me. How-why, does a person change like that? Did he think I was crazy? He never told me.

For months I couldn't sleep or eat. Having never been depressed, I didn't recognize the warning signs, but after losing 20 pounds in a month, I decided to see a doctor. Where upon, she prescribed anti-depressants and stipulated that if I weren't substantially better in two weeks I would be hospitalized.

Oh my GOD! How did I allow myself to get like this? How could this happen to me? When I heard the words *hospital* I thought, not only "*NO, but HELL NO!*" I won't allow this to happen! And at that moment I knew I had to save myself. I could no longer live in a toxic, negative environment that was literally making me sick. Armed with two forks, knives, spoons, dishes and rented furniture I moved into an apartment. I desperately wanted him to call. The first call would not come for over two months. I felt abandoned.

Deeply saddened, distraught and overwhelmed, I knew I had to get a handle on my situation as quickly as possible. Besides, I hate suffering and feeling miserable! So I sought the advice of an Asian guru asking him how to get myself back to my center and find my peace again. How do I heal my broken heart? How do I move on with grace? How do I see my husband as the good and decent man he was? Life served me a curve ball, a wild pitch and it hit me right between the eyes. Life as I knew it had changed forever.

The guru explained that walking meditation could help me heal from the inside out and bring me back into peace and harmony. He also told me that our body is like a battery. When we start opening our hearts we can become empathic. All I needed to do was make my battery larger. Walking mediation was the key.

Walking meditation didn't *feel* anything like sitting meditation. None of those dreamy, zoned-out feelings I *thought* was supposed to be meditation. I was fully awake, fully aware, and practicing outside.

Being hyper aware, I quickly realized I had stumbled onto something very powerful and profound. Literally, I began regaining my energy and emotional balance. I could see a subtle difference in my face and skin. Although I didn't understand all the benefits of walking meditation, all I really cared about was that I was feeling better! Within six months I was off of all meds and within a year my "battery" was bigger and I was less susceptible to the negative energies around me. I had regained my joy.

My story's not new. Lots of people go through divorce and most everyone will go through the dark night of the soul. But walking meditation is my foundation to help me stay healthy, slow the aging process and to help me understand myself and others better. Are we ever finished with life's challenges? I think not, but walking meditation is my *go-to* staple for living no matter what life throws my way and a skill set I encourage everyone to cultivate.

Cyndy Justice

Cyndy Justice is active in her community and is a connector of people in business and in life. She finds great satisfaction in helping businesses and individuals keep in touch and nurture relationships with the people who are important to them. She is a trainer in relationship marketing with a special emphasis on gratitude.

She is the founder of the initial chapter of Network Texas, now ten chapters strong. She has served in her local Chambers of Commerce as an ambassador and a board member. She is also an ambassador for a local medical ministry.

Learn more about Cyndy:

Website: www.cyndyjustice.com
Website: www.sendoutcards.com/cjustice
Email: cyndy@cyndyjustice.com
Social Media Links:
Facebook: facebook.com/cyndy.justice
LinkedIn: linkedin.com/pub/cyndy-justice/1/217/b34
Twitter: twitter.com/cyndyjustice
Instagram: instagram.com/just1ck
Google Plus: plus.google.com/+CyndyJustice

Chapter 5

GOD'S GRACE IS SUFFICIENT

By Cyndy Justice

I imagine you would have liked my husband, Dan. Though living with his grandmother provided stability for a few years, most of his home life was quite unstable. As a result, though very bright, Dan left school early and joined the US Merchant Marines. Traveling the world was a great adventure for a couple of years, but spending a short time in a Middle East hospital prompted him to reevaluate his life. He needed new direction.

Not shy of facing challenges, Dan enlisted in the Navy. He was stationed on a conventional submarine and became a diver. This was a new world, running miles and miles, diving in the icy waters of the North Sea, recovering torpedoes. I have always appreciated the importance and necessity of the submarine service, but volunteering for it? Having been invited to take a 'dependent's cruise' for about an hour, I truly came to appreciate the sacrifice submariners' make.

Because Dan hadn't completed his education, he did earn his GED and took advantage of every school that came his way in military and civilian life. He was organized and talented. What he didn't know he figured out, finding a better way to get things done. I had to call a repair guy only twice in the thirty-three years we were married.

He was thoughtful, remembering our anniversary and my birthday. Sometimes that was quite comical! When he had been traveling for business in Tyler, Texas, the Rose Capitol of the US, he bought a handful of beautiful roses wrapped in tissue paper. As I carefully unwrapped the flowers, all the petals fell off, making us chuckle. At least he remembered! He also had a good sense of humor and loved to tease waitresses and give them a hard time!

Though Dan was gone every other week, working in the oil industry offshore, Danny would get excited when Wednesday came around because Daddy was coming home. They were best buddies! Dan took as much time as he could with Danny when he was home, practicing baseball, teaching him helpful 'guy' skills, and teaching him to be thoughtful. Danny had great respect for Dan and may have had a difference of opinion from time to time, but once Dan spoke, that settled it. He was the rock of our family.

That all came to an end on February 4, 2005. Dan had done dangerous work with boilers, high voltage electricity, cranes, and offshore installations. I always knew someone might call and say that he had not survived an explosion or some other kind of industrial accident. I never dreamed, however, that we would be driving together, less than twenty miles from home, when I would lose him, my best friend. It was as though he was snatched away!

Since Dan was no longer working offshore, gone every other week, he had more time at home. We had decided to visit with some friends that Friday evening. I remember walking into their kitchen and handing the ice cream to our friend, Joe.

I don't remember anything for the next eight days. As we drove home, about 11 PM, we were struck head-on by a drunk driver, an adult in his 50's. He had been drinking beer all day and had consumed about 60 ounces of margaritas within three hours at a local

Mexican restaurant. His blood alcohol content was three times the legal maximum amount for Texas.

I didn't realize that automobiles had 'black boxes', similar to those in airplanes, but those 'boxes' showed that Dan had slowed down to about 20 miles per hour, after veering onto the guardrail, while other driver was traveling at about 70 miles per hour. It was as though we had hit a wall at 90 miles an hour.

Dan was killed instantly, and I was Life-Flighted about 50 miles to Memorial Hermann Hospital in Houston. I sustained a compound fracture of my left arm, head trauma, and impaired vision; I remained in a coma for about four days. The fractured arm required surgery, and the physicians had to drill a hole in my skull to relieve the pressure on my brain.

From the moment Danny learned about the wreck, he had to assume great responsibility. While trying to comprehend losing his dad, at the age of eighteen, he had to authorize my surgery, select the appropriate attire and casket for Dan, and arrange a funeral, with burial at Houston National Cemetery, dedicated to those who have served in the military.

God's grace was in evidence, however. Remarkably, I was hospitalized only ten days. My family came from Illinois and Rhode Island to be with Danny and spend time with me at the hospital. Friends and clients also came to stay with me, as I required 24-hour monitoring. It is surprising that, as a financial advisor at the time, I was able to carry on relatively sane conversations about some investments with my brother- in-law, and I even recognized a few people.

However, I couldn't understand why the man (a medical technician) walking through my room frequently, who I thought was Dan, didn't come talk with me. It required three or four occasions for my family to help me comprehend that I had lost Dan. I remember saying, "I guess I don't have a husband anymore."

Wise friends were able to quickly refer legal guidance to Danny and my brother-in-law because of our position as victims of drunk driving. There was a possibility, even though I was entirely not at fault, that I might have been required to give a deposition. That would have been extremely stressful, but God graciously prevented that from happening.

Fridays were always trying. It seemed that, invariably, there would be something in the mail to cause concern, such as the $10,000 Life Flight invoice. I knew I couldn't inquire about that until Monday, so I had another opportunity to trust God with the result, which eventually, was a significant discount.

While my sister and brother-in –law and parents stayed with me for several weeks, I finally suggested that they return home, so I could determine if I could carry on my life without their assistance. Fortunately, Danny was very attentive and continued to live with me to help in any way possible. While trying to work and go to college, but having great difficulty sleeping, he drove for me, shopped for me, cared for me. Even with his help, living on my own was challenging at first, as I was dealing with memory loss. For a few weeks, I made a list every evening of everything I needed to do the next day, including washing clothes, to make sure I wouldn't forget.

After regular surgery, laser and acupuncture therapy, my arm required physical and occupational therapy for months. Because I was not able to drive, wonderful friends volunteered to drive me to every appointment, whether they were local or in Houston.

The initial optical evaluation was that I might never drive again, but I learned to place a tiny patch on my glasses to temporarily block the double vision in my left eye. Since I had lost peripheral vision on the left side as well, by working around the double vision, I didn't have to contend with two visual challenges at the same time. About nine months after the wreck, I got up the courage to venture out of my driveway and began driving cautiously around our neighborhood circle. After I mastered that seven-tenths of a mile, I conquered the local roads in one-mile increments. Two months later I navigated the thirty-seven mile drive to church, with Danny along for reassurance.

What are the residual results of our life-altering experience?"

Bad decisions limit future options."

Every spring Danny and I speak to high school juniors and seniors about the consequences of the decisions they make, particularly drinking and driving, in a program called Shattered Lives. Students volunteer, with their parents' permission, to be part of the program.

Because someone dies every 15 minutes in the US because of an alcohol-related incident, a volunteer is pulled out of class every 15 minutes, wearing a T-shirt that says 'Living Dead' and remains out of school for the rest of the day.

Parents of these students write obituaries in honor of their children, which are posted in the halls throughout the school. Other students participate as 'victims' of a wreck. They are positioned in vehicles that have actually been wrecked, 'made-up' to look injured. The 'drunk 'driver is 'arrested' by local police, brought before a Justice of the Peace, and sentenced to jail, where their parents identify them. Victims who have 'died' are placed in body bags and taken away in hearses. 'Injured victims' are taken in ambulances to hospitals where their parents also identify them. Occasionally, Life Flight will agree to participate and transport a 'victim' to the hospital.

In the evening, the students gather for a retreat where they hear speakers who have had experience in drinking and driving incidents.

That is where Danny and I tell our story. The students can truly relate to Danny, as he was their age when all of this happened to him. At the close of his talk, Danny gives the students his phone number with these instructions. If they are ever in a situation where they have been drinking and need to get home, they can call him. He won't lecture them; he will just get them home safely. One student has taken him up on that offer. Danny had to drive an hour to take that student three blocks, but they weren't driving or relying on someone else in an impaired state to get him or her home. It was a privilege to do that.

The evening of the retreat ends with a thought-provoking exercise. Before going to sleep, the students write letters to their parents as though it was their final communication – "The things I never had a chance to tell you." The following day, there is an assembly for all junior and senior students who hear additional speakers, and then the students return to their families.

Young people tend to think they're invincible! I always remind them that, when they drive, it is not all about them! They need to think of the actions they take before they drive, and while they drive (texting). They are excited about becoming adults, but I remind them that they need to make adult decisions and take responsibility for their actions. The guy that hit us did not!

If they drink and drive, resulting in a wreck, it is not an accident! It is their fault and they can blame no one else! I always remind them that bad decisions limit future options. If we can reach at least one student by sharing our story and showing them that the decisions they make can be a matter of life and death, we will have made a difference in one person's life.

I still struggle with visual challenges. I only drive in the evening when it's necessary and only to the nearest town, five miles away. I just can't see in the dark! I also have depth perception difficulties.

I have a difficult time determining how much distance there is between me and other vehicles and have to be very cautious in changing lanes. As a result, I rarely drive in traffic.

Unfortunately, I might step on the cat's tail or stumble over the dog because I don't see them, or I might knock a glass off the counter with my left hand. If I walk with someone, I ask them to walk on my right side. If they walk on my left, I might step on their feet.

Danny misses wonderful times with his dad and conversations about the important things in life. The greatest heartache was not having Dan present on the most special day in his life- his wedding day. Dan would have loved Taylor, Danny's wife. She is beautiful and talented, but he also would have teased her as often as he could. He would have been a really fun grandpa.

I also changed careers. When my dad passed away, I invited my mom to live with me because she had some major health concerns. She wasn't a burden at all, but her health would require more of my attention. Investments had become more of a challenge, not behaving the way they should with government intrusion and other factors. Remaining in the industry would have required me to continue to keep up with changes in the investment world, including tax law and compliance, and that would mean less time to focus on Mom.

While an advisor, I had been introduced to a phenomenal relationship-marketing tool that could help me keep in touch with my clients and prospects to let them know that I was thinking of them and that I appreciated them. The system was designed to help people act on their promptings. What is a prompting? It's a thought that guides us, reminds us to tell someone they are important to us, they are special, we need to keep in touch. Instead of going to a greeting card or grocery store and then to the post office, I could compose customized greeting cards online. The company would print, stuff, stamp and mail a real, physical greeting card that I had created with personalized pictures, and my own handwriting font and signature if I chose, and that card would arrive in the recipient's mailbox with a gift, if I had so designated. All I had to do was create the card and click 'send card.' Building and maintaining relationships are important to me, and this would allow me to help connect people in business and in life, with almost no paperwork and very simple compliance. I could also invite people to work with me. It would leverage my time and efforts, and I could help them build a business while I built mine.

Does it work? Because Danny sent Taylor one of these cards with a heartfelt message, I now have a fabulous daughter- in-law. I always knew that my agenda for the rest of my life was not necessarily God's agenda, but I also thought that thirty-three years with Dan was just the beginning. God had other plans. He could have taken me when He took Dan, but He has something else in mind for me, however long that might be. I'm not sure exactly what He has planned, but Danny and Taylor have given me permission to teach their children, whenever they have them, Texas history and the Bible. I appreciate veterans and would like to help them in some way and would like to extend my help with the Shattered Lives programs. I'd also like to use my experiences to encourage and support other widows. I am here, totally by God's grace, and in whatever I do I want to honor Him.

Eric Wilson

Eric Wilson is President of I Sell Health, Inc. A full Service insurance agency in the Chicago Area. He is licensed in Illinois, Indiana, Iowa, Wisconsin, Ohio, South Carolina, Georgia, Texas and North Dakota. He has been in the industry since 1991. Wilson opened his own agency in 2004. He has been featured in *The Suit Magazine, LifeHealth Pro and Benefits Pro,* as well as, ABC, NBC, CNN and Fox. He has also written the "Guest Editorial" multiple times for *California Broker Magazine.* He specializes in individual health insurance, Medicare and Tax-Free Retirement Solutions.

You can learn more about Eric:
Website: www.isellhealth.com
Website: www.examiner.com/health-insurance-29-in-chciago/eric-wilson
Email: isellhealth@gmail.com
Social Media Links
LinkedIn: www.linkedin.com/pub/eric-wilson/2/aaa/450
Twitter: @isellhealth

Chapter 6

SOMETIME YOU JUST NEED A LITTLE PUSH

By Eric Wilson

I grew up in a small town in New Jersey, just outside of Philadelphia, Pa. In 1987, I graduated from tiny St. James High School in Carney's Point. I loved the small high school. Being a two-sport athlete and a National Honor Society student kind of made me a hometown hero. It was a great thing to be a part of growing up. I then went to a Liberal Arts College, Western Maryland College in a town called Westminster. It was a tough first year. I went from an All-Conference football player to playing my first year. Academics were even tougher. I never really learned how to study in high school so my grades were not so good. At the first semester break I had knee surgery from a football injury and struggled through the second semester, again not a great year for me. I spent the summer break rehabilitating my knee and in summer school. Somehow it all clicked after that summer, my grades came up and I returned to the gridiron, being awarded the colleges' most courageous athlete award and graduating in 1991.

In 1991, it was a tough economy. My Dad was out of work at the time so when I took my first job I did it with mixed emotions. The salary was low and it was in Washington, DC where the cost of living was high. I was not sure I really wanted to take the job but felt with my

Dad out of work and my brother still in college I really should not live at home and be a burden to the family. I moved to Maryland and began working for a small insurance replacement car rental company for a salary of $15,000 per year. My rent to live in Maryland, about an hour north of DC, was over $7000 per year. I survived eating a lot of macaroni and rice for about a year. While it was a tough year it was a good lesson in survival. I worked hard at the job and really learned the business. Since I did not know anyone in town I got to the office early and stayed late. About a year later I got promoted and moved to Columbus, Ohio. Columbus was a troubled market for this company and it was losing about $20,000 a month when I arrived. In the beginning I still was not making much money, but I was single so I did not have huge expenses and rent was lower in Ohio than DC, so was the cost of living. It took about two years of 10 to 12 hour days to make that location successful. It became one of the top offices in the country. I spent seven years with the same company in Ohio and met my wife along the way.

I was promoted again in 1999 and moved to the Chicago area. This became another personal economic challenge. While I got a small pay raise to move, it did not keep up with the cost of living. Something in hindsight I wished I would have researched a little more before agreeing to the move. It put some strains on my family life. We were not making much money and my wife was away from her family in Ohio, for the first time. We had to change our lifestyle a little bit. We stopped going out to dinner. I was traveling for work usually 3 to 4 days a week. My wife knew nobody and I was not around, it was tough on her, she is a strong person, but it wore me down knowing that she was unhappy. It was exhausting! Part of me wanted to quit, sell our new house and go back to Ohio. I guess more of me said, Eric, you have never quit anything in your life and you are not going to start now. After a tough year of kicking and scratching to earn a decent living, the company hit some financial troubles and after almost ten years with the company, it was time to move on. It was a tough time because I thought I might work for that company forever, but the timing was right to move on.

I spent the next five years with a fantastic company and made more money than I had ever made. I, again, was working in a troubled market, but this company gave me flexibility to do what I needed to do to make the market successful. I had more support from the home office that I had ever had before. My Regional Manager basically said he could get me whatever I needed. So I hired a lot of my guys from the car rental company I had worked with previously and we built a successful team and market. Sadly, this company too was hit with some financial difficulties and filed for bankruptcy. They started downsizing throughout the company. First the operations managers went away then the sales managers. This was about six months after my second son was born. For the first time in my life I found myself unemployed. Great timing, a week before Christmas! After almost fifteen years and two companies that had gone up in smoke, I realized I could not take the corporate culture any more, fifteen years of work and only a little bit of money in a 401(K) to show for it. I had always wanted to start my own business but was kind of afraid of not having a steady paycheck. It was kind of a blessing that I lost my job, as I no longer had to fear the loss of a paycheck. I did not have one anymore.

The thought of running my own company intrigued me even back as far as the days of selling gum in elementary school and cutting lawns in high school, but the question now was what could I do now that I could turn into a lucrative business quickly? Many of my friends were starting home remodeling business or landscaping businesses. I am not real good with tools so I eliminated those ideas. I considered buying a franchise, but startup costs were high, and I was not sure I wanted to take out a loan at that point in my life. My corporate career had been in the insurance replacement industry with car rental and auto glass, which ultimately led me to look at insurance for my business.

As I started to look at the industry, I looked at property and casualty (home and auto etc.) insurance. I talked to State Farm, American Family and Farmers. The issue again was startup costs and cash reserve. When working on commissions for insurance products like this the monthly could be as little as $25 or $30 per month, which when you get enough can be an incredible life. But, it is a slow process and you have to rent office space and eventually hire a staff. I did not want to take on the debt that would be required. I also knew it would take five years to be profitable. That was more time than I had.

I got into the health insurance business. I figured I could start this with fairly low overhead; I could work out of the house and not need a staff. So my company was born in December of 2004. I really figured with my sales skills I would be making money in no time! Well, starting a health insurance agency is just like starting any other business. It started with ups and downs. I would be really busy selling health plans, but because I was busy selling, I was not prospecting. I would have 3 good weeks then 3 bad weeks, it was a tough balancing act. I remember I had a spell where I went six weeks without a sale, which meant about 8 weeks without a check. After about six months, I had to take on a job to pay the bills, while I tried to get my business going. I hated these odd jobs; they took time away from my business. I had to do it though because I had a family to feed. I was working from 6–8AM on my business, then 8–3 on a job, then 3 to 8 or 9PM back on my business. This was tough on the family, I had two kids starting to grow up that I didn't get to see due to having to put the time in to build the business and support the family. After about a year of the odd jobs, I was able to focus full time on my insurance business. I was not making much, but enough to survive. It took about four years to start making money on a consistent basis. Part of that was learning how to market my business. Part of it was time management. Some of it was finding the right product mix. Then the tough part was keeping the clients I had on the books. Staying on top of them, offering them a new plan at renewal time before they thought about calling someone else. Once I got it going I believed it was the best business in the world. When 2009 came around I had customers, money, time and products, it was awesome!

In 2010 the Patient Protection Affordable Care Act (PPACA) otherwise known as Obamacare passed. The ACA put a few of my top insurance carriers with good pricing and commissions out of business. This law then forced the insurance carriers to reduce commissions. They were actually cut in half. I took almost a $50,000 pay cut. Because of the commission cuts, I had to cut back advertising, which further cut into sales. It was becoming a vicious cycle. I had to make a decision. Do I stay in business? Do I dare go back to corporate America? Do I expand the product lines? The latter is what I did. I got some more certifications as well as a property and casualty license. I tried to migrate into different products like life insurance and annuities or even property and casualty. Sure I sold some and did ok with it, but I always found that I missed health insurance which I knew so well. I decided that in order to continue to be successful in the health insurance business I had to understand the new health care law. I read every page of it. I tried to absorb as much of it as I could. To get more clients I had to become an expert on all things "Obamacare". Sometimes I felt like I spent too much time reading and studying the law and not enough time selling products.

While so many health insurance brokers left the business, I persevered and followed my passion and stayed the course of health insurance. In January of 2014, when the bulk of "Obamacare" was implemented commissions were again cut by 40%, but the underwriting was gone, so I captured some business that I otherwise would not have, but it was still a lot more work for a lot less money. I had to really understand the client's needs at this point. I had to change the operating model because with the reduction in commissions I had to see more clients. Technology helped. I really reduced the number of face to face clients I met with. The drive time was often times an hour or more each way. I could not invest that time anymore.

Web conferencing has become a huge part of what I do now. I save a minimum of 10 hours a week in drive time. This allows me more time for marketing and selling products. Also more time to offer more products to the clients who need them. The game does not stop, only the rules change. After about 4 years of making significantly less money, commissions are almost back to the 2009 levels. I expect to exceed those levels in 2016. One of the great lines I ever heard came from the Reverend Robert Schuller. He said, "tough times don't last, but tough people do."

Fion Bain

Fiona is a Certified Professional Life Coach who is passionate about life coaching. She brings her positivity and love for life to her coaching and supports people in being well, fulfilled and vibrantly alive. Life coaching fulfills Fiona's purpose -- to help other women become empowered in their own lives, to see their own radiance and hear their own inner guidance. Women who are ready to create a life that is true and rich, full of meaning, pleasure, inner peace, with a clear mind and heart, at a stage in their life where they are putting themselves first.

Learn more about Fiona:
Website: www.fionabain.com
Email: fiona@fionabain.com
Social Media Links:
LinkedIn: https://www.linkedin.com/pub/fiona-bain/14/94a/109
Facebook: https://www.facebook.com/fiona.bain.39
Twitter: https://twitter.com/CoachWithFiona
Pinterest: http://www.pinterest.com/fionabain39/

Chapter 7

HOW I LEARNED TO FLY

By Fiona Bain

Have you ever had the rug pulled out from underneath you due to divorce, job loss, or death of a close loved one? Or, are you like some people who haven't had a life-defining catalyst, as much as a nagging thought that there must be more? The reality is that this doesn't have to be the end of your life as you know it...instead, it can be the beginning of a new, fabulously fun and enjoyable life. I have learned firsthand that there is more to life than what you may be living right now. I want to connect with women, in particular, who are beginning to ask "Now What?" or "What About Me?" Many of my clients have reached the point in their lives where they have accomplished their goals and were expecting to feel very different from what they are experiencing in this stage of their lives. When they hired me they had been questioning their future because they knew they wouldn't be happy if they stayed on their current flight plan. They knew that something had to change. They needed something to shift and were ready to take a leap, an action step that would help them get back in touch with who they really are and determine what they wanted their lives to look like.

My Search Begins

I grew up in Queens, New York with my younger brother and my English born parents. As a young married couple they had immigrated to the United States in search of a better life. Looking back, I wonder if that quest for a better life was somehow instilled in me as well. I note that because I never felt content or satisfied with where I was. I was always searching for more. The funny thing is, in all my searching, I never took the time to stop and figure out what I was searching for. I made decisions based on information in front of me at the time and my interpretation of my circumstances. I realize now that we all have some calling within us, we each have gifts. I wonder if in some way, somehow, this is what I was looking for—the "thing" that was pulling me forward. I was unknowingly in search of my gifts, my purpose, my meaning. It wasn't until I lost my job that I stopped to reflect and to figure it out. Looking back, I've come to understand that there were three key intersections in my life that, if I had mapped them differently, may have accelerated my journey to happiness much earlier in my life. At the time of each juncture I didn't have the clarity to figure it all out, but eventually I did.

My First Major Juncture

When I went to college, I wanted more than anything to be a marine biologist. I loved the ocean, marine animals, and was a huge Jacques Cousteau fan. I applied and was accepted to the State University of New York @ Stony Brook and set out taking the required classes to become a Marine Biologist. Life was good....until the day I had a conversation with my parents and they told me that no one ever gets a job as a Marine Biologist and they were not willing to support me if I was unable to get a job. That one conversation held enough power to get me to change my degree plan. I declared Economics as my degree. This was an early indicator of my tendency to do things for others, versus trusting myself to make the right decision. To go from Marine Biology to Economics is quite the change. I am not the only one to have done this, but it is an indicator of the power that we give others in our lives. After college, ironically, I was struggling to find a job, which was really painful to me. My whole reason for getting an Economics degree was to be able to find a job, and here I was without one. I started looking in to other things that I could do for a living. Along with wanting to be a Marine Biologist, I had always wanted to fly….so I thought, why not join the Navy and become a pilot. The funny thing is I never followed through with applying to be a pilot. Admittedly, I was afraid….. I was afraid of the dunk tank, I was afraid of failure and I was afraid to go it alone. I did well in the Navy, was promoted, and given more and more responsibility. Ultimately, however, I didn't feel that it was the best fit for me and decided to leave active duty. When I told my Executive Officer, he was shocked and offered me Post Graduate School….he asked "is there anything I can do or say to get you to stay in?" He relied on me heavily, but I knew that I wanted more freedom; I, wanted to get out and do something completely different. I spent a few years doing small part-time jobs along with being in the Navy Reserve. I continued to do well in the Navy Reserve and was eventually promoted to the rank of Commander.

I realized that I needed to make more money and to do that I knew that I had to go back to school to get a Master's Degree. When I made this decision, the only two degrees that I considered were a law degree (like my brother) or an MBA. It was at this point that intersection number two appears. Why didn't I stop here and figure out what would have been the best fit for me? Turns out, neither one of those were the best choice for me. I see that now, but I didn't then. I went to the University of Connecticut and got my MBA. What would it have meant to my life if I stopped and figured out what I truly wanted to be when I grew up. What prevented me from looking deeper into what it was that I truly I wanted?

Thankfully, I Was Fired!

After getting my MBA, I worked in corporate America for 13 years until I was fortunate enough to be let go as part of my companies downsizing. I say fortunate because as scary and uncertain as my future was, finally I would take the time to figure out what I wanted to be doing with my life. This was Intersection Number Three.

Don't get me wrong, when I was given notice in October of 2010 that I no longer had a job, I was mad, hurt, and shocked. How could they be laying me off? After the shock wore off, I finally stopped to think about what I wanted to do. What would make me truly happy? For more than 5 years I had been daydreaming about becoming a Life Coach. I felt that becoming a Life Coach would allow me to do the things I knew were important to me, empowering others, motivating and alleviating pain and suffering, giving back. I hadn't pursued it because I was the steady paycheck and the healthcare provider for my family. How could I give all of that up? Yet, here was my opportunity. The decision to leave corporate had been made by someone else, now I needed to figure out what it was that I wanted to do. Continue on in a career I no longer enjoyed or set off for some uncharted adventures. The opportunity to be in charge of my own destiny was alluring….was this what I had been searching for all along? A way to help, give back and live a truly authentic life?

What is it about humans that keeps some of us banging our heads against the wall, or doing the same things expecting different results? What is it that has to happen for us to get knocked off of the path we are on? For some, it might be reaching a certain age; for others, it happens when the discomfort becomes too unbearable. For me it was both, at age 49 I realized I had become comfortable being uncomfortable but I was no longer willing to suffer anymore. I knew what that felt like and was not okay staying there.

Here was the opportunity for me to create the life I had dreamed of, to get a job where I could help other people live truly empowered lives. I knew that helping others was my passion....I had been doing that all along, but now I wanted to really get out there and help more people. I hired a Life Coach to see what it was like and to see if it was truly something I would want to do. I wanted to get it right this time. I wanted to takeoff on a flight plan that would be fulfilling, rewarding and beneficial to others, and that wasn't going to be me going back to corporate America. I knew I wanted to help other women who were feeling like I was....stuck in a life and they weren't even sure of how they got there. Working with my coach, we discussed a lot of things, I identified my values, came up with my life purpose, and the work together confirmed that becoming a Certified Life Coach would be a great fit for me. Finally, I had taken the time to figure out what I truly wanted and found something I loved...coaching!

Discovering a Life of Passion and Purpose

I enrolled in the Coaching Program at Institute for Professional Excellence in Coaching (iPEC). The wonderful thing about iPEC was the introduction to working with supportive individuals. People who truly wanted to help me and weren't coming from a place of lack or fear. They know that the resources are endless and that there is plenty to go around. What a difference from my other jobs. Previously I had worked with individuals who were only interested in their getting ahead, and here I was in an environment where others wanted to help me succeed. It was incredible. Since my certification, the best part about my new career is the transformations I see in myself and in my clients. It is such an honor to be on this journey with them. The growth, happiness and fulfillment that my clients experience is amazing and something I hold dear. All the answers are within us. It is just a matter of me asking the right questions, holding a safe place, removing judgment, challenging them at times and teasing out the answers.

"You were born with potential. You were born with goodness and trust. You were born with ideals and dreams. You were born with greatness. You were born with wings. You are not meant for crawling, so don't. You have wings. Learn to use them and fly." – Rumi

Maybe this was the flying that I dreamed about….it isn't until we expand our horizons that we learn about other opportunities, other ways of being. Until that happens, we just keep doing the same things over and over again….just like the movie Groundhog Day with Bill Murray. What I have found, and what my clients find as well, is that there are many more opportunities out there than we realize. That if we spend the time to stop and figure out what it is we want, we will live a much more fulfilled life. I am happily married, with a wonderful daughter and we do all the things that bring us joy and fulfillment. Life is truly amazing, and I couldn't do it without my clients, my coaches and my partners. And of course my husband and my daughter….they truly are the best part of this journey

My wish for you is that you stop and make whatever changes you need to make to live a full life. "You have wings. Learn to use them and fly!"

Monique T. LaCour

Monique T. LaCour is the Principal of *Career Management Services.* She has contributed to nationally-published career development books and frequently serves as a guest speaker on a variety of career- and business-related topics. Monique also serves as an executive coach and mentor to budding entrepreneurs and loves volunteering with charitable organizations. She grew up in the Army (never call her a "brat", though!), is a graduate of the University of Houston and now calls Houston, Texas home.

Monique's passion is helping entrepreneurs and other business professionals find meaning and fulfillment in their work. You will often hear her say "You have a purpose. Mine is to help you EXCEL at it!"

Learn more about Monique:
Website: www.CenterStageGroup.com
Email: CoachM@CenterStageGroup.com
Phone: 713-998-6985
Social Media Links:
Facebook: www.facebook.com/HoustonBusinessLounge
LinkedIn: www.linkedin.com/in/moniquelacour

Chapter 8

SORRY, THAT'S JUST NOT NEGOTIABLE!

By Monique T. LaCour

I grew up in a military family with parents that taught us to believe in ourselves and always do our best, no matter what. Set a goal, work your plan and NEVER negotiate when it comes to your values. What made them so believable is that they really walked the talk. My dad always talked about the fact that he really wanted his daughters to go to college. He grew up in an era where men typically worked and women stayed at home to take care of the kids. He realized, however, that if the provider takes off and the homemaker has no income and skills, things were going to go downhill fast. He just didn't want that for his daughters. Of course my parents wanted all of us (two boys, two girls, with me being the youngest) to be successful. Dad was especially concerned about his daughters being self-sufficient. So, that's exactly what I did. I graduated high school and then came to Houston to attend college eventually obtaining my degree from the University of Houston. Little did I know that his concerns would be put to the test in my life...

In 1998, I found myself separated from the man I considered my very best friend. I started Career Management Services in 1993, in addition to helping my husband launch his financial services firm, splitting my time between the businesses and in my full-time job as an IT consultant. Looking back, my trying to juggle a corporate job, two startup companies and a new baby was a lofty goal! I don't remember getting a full night's sleep for many years! All of a sudden, I had to do the juggling alone. Going forward, it was going to be just me and my 6 year old son.

I wanted to keep life for my son as "normal" as possible, so that meant that I had to plan work around his school hours. I wanted to drop him off at school in the morning, participate in school activities when needed, and then pick him up when school let out. No exceptions. Day care was an option, but I just had this strong desire to enjoy as much of those precious years as I could, because I knew they would pass by quickly. I was going to have to be creative though. Corporate America back then was not as forgiving when it came to flexible work hours as they are now. You were expected to show up at 8am and leave no earlier than 5pm.

I took a look at all of the skills I had collected over the years and separated them into two groups; 1-"they need me there to do this", 2-"they don't need me there to do this". Because my technical work involved developing software applications and did not require me to be on site most of the time, I started negotiating working onsite between 9am and 2pm, then offsite the remainder of the hours, which still offered companies the 40 hours they wanted. My first "bite" came from a major oil and gas company that did not have a policy of allowing independent contractors to work offsite. However, they had a staff that was interested in using a technology with which I had considerable experience. I convinced them that I could give them the solution they needed in the time frame they required. They agreed to give it a try and with just my laptop and cell phone I was now free to work both my plans! That was supposed to be a 5-month contract. It ended up lasting almost a year. I then used this assignment to negotiate the next, even lengthier contract, then, in the years to follow, created a portfolio of success stories that helped me secure flexible assignments for many years.

It was so uncommon at the time, I almost couldn't believe that I was able to work from home/coffee shops/out of state and still be paid the same or better salary as I would have if I had been tied to a desk. Best of all, my clients neither knew the difference, nor cared. I always delivered more than was expected. The best thing about it all was that I was able to do what was most important to me; be available for my son. Nothing felt better than to being able to pick him up from school, help him with his homework and have a little play time before most people got home from work.

One of my first major clients was a recruiting firm that I had worked with as a consultant. I talked them into letting me update their resumes and conduct their technical interviews for a monthly fee. I then targeted other recruiting firms, consultants and business professionals and provided a fee-based resume and faxing service (ok, it was high-tech back then) for them. I would usually meet clients during lunch, after work hours, or on the weekends. Eventually, I was starting to generate steady income, which helped me get Career Management Services on its feet.

Don't get me wrong, this was hardly a cake walk! Sometimes meeting a client for coffee meant having my son seated at the next table with homework, a snack and a hot chocolate. On a couple of occasions I would teach late-night classes and have my son sitting at a computer with the other students (with the blessing of the class and staff, of course!). Thankfully, during this time, my parents were able to baby sit from after school until I picked him up, which meant driving almost an hour to their house, then another hour home. It seemed as though I was working more hours than when I was married! My most vivid memories are of the countless, coffee-filled all-nighters I had to pull in order to get everything done. But that was ok. My plan was more important!

I eventually lessened my technical work and began increasing my coaching and training services, providing both in-person and virtual coaching services to job applicants and corporate clients. By 2000, I decided that Career Management Services was going to be my full-time focus. I wanted to be able to use my experiences to help others, especially moms, create the careers that align with their values and give them a sense of purpose. One of the biggest lessons I learned about my business was that the clients will tell you which direction to take, which means your business will always be a work in progress. So, in time, I added leadership training and executive coaching services to my business. That is what I have been doing to date and I've never looked back!

But here is the unexpected thing that made it all worthwhile. When my son was only 12 years old and as we were driving home from having dinner out that evening, I noticed that he was much quieter than usual. He stared out of the car window, then all of a sudden asked, "Mom, when you used to work home all of the time, did you do that to be with me?" I never told him that. I answered, "I certainly did, kid!" He got quiet again, then said, "Thanks Mom". I think of that moment often and it still brings tears to my eyes. That is why I am such an advocate of doing what you love, being creative about making it work and not budging on what's most important to you. It was all so worth it!

Well, my son's a smart, handsome, well-adjusted college man now and Mom doesn't have to drive him to and from school anymore. But every now and then when we talk about the old days, he can articulate what those years meant to him and I get a little insight into his young world. Sometimes I'll hear him say, "I had a great childhood!" or "Those were good times!" and I don't think he realizes how precious those words are to me!

I'm sharing my story to encourage moms everywhere who are struggling to care for their families to never, ever give up. NEVER stop growing, learning and keeping your mind open to finding ways to work your plan, no matter how hard things get or how little you think your kids notice. Trust me, they do. And this mom will be here to hold your hand through the journey and cheer you on!

Nathan Dewsbury, MSc

Nathan Dewsbury is the unique cross between scientist and businessman. He combines vast laboratory experience and vaccine development with his successful career in consultative sales. This makes him one of the most valued Regional Managers in the Animal Health industry.

His professional and personal interests have been directed to improve animal health in North America. His multiple West Nile Vaccine publications and appointment to the NIAA Bovine Committee are just a few accomplishments of his talent.

Nathan lives in Texas with his wife Stacy and their son Wyatt where he enjoys spending time training dogs.

Learn more about Nathan:
Website: www.linkedin.com/in/nathandewsbury
Email: natx88@hotmail.com

Chapter 9

ONE STAR AT A TIME

By Nathan Dewsbury

Imagine for a moment lying on the ground and staring up into a clear night sky brimming with stars. You can see there is so much out there that is full of wonder and possibility. Then you realize the reality of the situation: you are infinitely far away from those stars and you won't experience any of it because you are stuck on the ground! This is how I describe my experience of living in a trailer park when I was a child. Growing up a poor trailer park kid, I never had a plan or a road map—or rather a star chart, I suppose—let alone the guidance of how to use those tools to achieve success.

It was rough on a child's mindset, growing up with the reality that you were at the perceived bottom of society. This affected the friends I had and limited my childhood experiences. The fear of negative judgment from my schoolmates if they saw my living conditions was more than enough reason for me to hide my reality. This was my burden and my world until I graduated from high school. I could have easily given in to the circumstances of my life. I felt victimized and that I was being held back for no fault of my own. This was my mindset until I made a life-changing decision while I was still in my childhood. I decided that I would not let my start in life hold me back from greatness. This is the seed that would grow into the foundation of my success.

As if being a poor trailer park kid wasn't hard enough, the addition of a learning barrier also challenged me. I was diagnosed with attention deficit disorder—ADD—early in my school years. Learning the value of hard work helped both me and those who supported me through a learning bottleneck during elementary school. Applying new learning tactics and practices helped me compensate for an alternative learning style and furthered my ability to become self-sufficient. It was then that I saw the first fruits of my labor. Refinement of those early learning habits evolved my abilities in my college education years, which enabled further educational accomplishments by the time I graduated from college in 2004. Thus the development of my guiding principle in life—which became to learn, apply, and refine— came into my consciousness. The landmark example of my principle becoming relevant was when I became the first in my family to obtain a college degree. Once I learned the power of this principle, it became infectious and I was off to apply it in every aspect of my life.

After graduating I spent four successful years working in vaccine development, completed two scientific publications, accomplished my goals as a competitive weight lifter, gained recognition as a gifted dog trainer, and became a canine nutrition aficionado. I was then accepted into a dual-degree graduate program at Texas A&M University and was in what seemed like a stable nine-year relationship with a woman I had dated since high school. We were engaged to be married. The world seemed in line with my ambitions and I knew where I wanted to be in five years.

It was 2008 when my next challenge presented itself. Over the Thanksgiving holiday, I discovered that my fiancé and I had grown apart. Unbeknownst to me, she was leading a second life while I supported her during medical school. The outcome of her failure to end the double life was as painful as any divorce, just a lot less paperwork. Having lived together for seven years qualified our relationship as a common law marriage in Texas, and that carried the same stipulations on personal property as divorce. I was left with an empty house, literally, and a truck. I was soon on the emotional roller coaster that comes with such a monumental life change.

This was the beginning of a new evolution on my journey. It was a chaotic time, and the whiplash of emotional highs and lows was mentally exhausting. Some very dark outlooks on life and the meaning of things took me to rock bottom, and I felt even greater anger than I felt when I was growing up poor. I could immediately sympathize with people who had been there before. It's the kind of membership that can leave you jaded, lost, and if unchecked can control all aspects of your life. Learning to work through those emotions and thoughts was life altering!

Despite the dark days that took me there, this change was the equivalent of a renaissance of new ideas and outlooks on life, and on the increased value in seeking experiences to enrich my life. I found new vigor to tackle problems head on, to learn from discomfort and not shy away. I applied new practices to manage my emotional changes through productive outlets. Writing, poetry, and personal development helped me move past disillusionment and trust in relationships again.

And so in 2011, I had recovered from divorce, graduated with two master's degrees, and re-entered the work force as a more confident single man. I was early in my career as an up-and-coming salesman traveling across West Texas calling on livestock feed companies. Driving around the vastness that is West Texas gave me a lot of time to think and plan things that I would implement later in my life. Of the many things that continued to run through my mind was the thought of all I could accomplish if I had more time, more money, and fewer distractions. I understood myself enough to know that it would take drastic actions to make that scenario a reality. I downsized my life by loosening my grip on material objects and the cognitive needs attached to them. This approach gave me more money and freed up some time, while also removing distractions that did not enrich my life. I sold everything I had accumulated in my house over the last three years. Nothing was off limits to accomplish my goal of becoming a "gypsy." I sold my guns, furniture, tools, my treasured 1964 Chevelle, and anything else that was not nailed down. I paid off as much debt as possible and used the money from my sales to buy a travel trailer.

This became my new home for the next year and a half. I moved it wherever my work and personal travels took me. I lived near lakes, rivers, and frequented RV parks near three or four major cities in Texas. I had already learned from previous trips, living minimalistically in a cot and tent for two-week stints that this was going to be a challenging endeavor, but the application of a gypsy lifestyle on a permanent basis was an obvious next step to prove myself. The first 30 days of my less-luxurious lifestyle were hard, but the ability to overcome the mental hardships perceived from the decision was the hardest. Refinement of my abilities over time and self-discipline soon became my new normal. A true adventure in self-discovery of my limits!

Just as I had purposefully decided to live a gypsy lifestyle to allow myself to grow, I purposefully decided to further develop my capacity to manage fear—or at least my aversions to fear. I'm not just talking about fear of change, fear of relationships, or fear of unicorns, but the fear of taking risks on decisions that could make meaningful impacts on my life. My gypsy lifestyle helped me shed layers of fear of change and enabled me to remain open to opportunity. I realized I was in control and free to do anything, anytime, and anywhere I chose. As a result, I now view the initial fleeting feeling of fear associated with situations when it comes time to make real decisions to implement, either in my life personally or professionally, as a positive! Rather than allowing the uncertainty of risk to cloud my choices, I embrace the fear and the risk. It was at this time that a good friend and I started a small company in the livestock feed manufacturing industry. I used this opportunity to create a specialized approach in preservation control products and also create testing programs around that specialization to monitor biological contaminant levels.

A year later I was still a gypsy, completely self-employed, applying my new skills, and fully involved in the everyday operations of running a business. I was getting to incorporate my science and business experience into my company when an amazing opportunity presented itself. An animal diagnostic company, headquartered in Switzerland, was looking for someone to re-launch their U.S. business division after five consecutive years of declining sales. I wondered, "Why should I consider this change?" I was already making good money. I was my own boss with no one trying to micromanage me and I had full creative control of my business. My question was answered by my own guiding principle. I needed to seize this opportunity to advance my learning in another segment of the animal health industry. Since I had already conditioned myself not to let my fear of change negatively impact my decisions, I easily accepted the job.

My reward for tackling another risk to learn animal diagnostics profoundly expanded my knowledge base in test development, test application, point of usage, and government regulation policies. Additional opportunities with this company allowed me to grow my international business experience and my worldwide network. By applying my new knowledge and skills along with even more hard work, I helped to stabilize the five-year sales decline, revamped the operational workflows, and built new and existing customer relationships to grow neglected parts of the business. Refinement of my unique blend of science and business knowledge was further demonstrated by transitioning the U.S. division through a merger with the largest animal health company in the world; while also maintaining 100% of the business's performance goals. After the merger, I was retained as a U.S. Regional Manager and continued to set new levels of achievement in my capacity.

Events in my life have shown me that there's no reason not to go for your goals. I've discovered that instead there are many good reasons to go for your goals: adventure, enjoyment, fulfillment, unexpected opportunities, personal growth, and the joy of meeting people that you would not have known had you not reached for your goals. Now I look forward to the future challenges of building my own personal empire. My practice to never stop learning, combined with the ability to apply what I learn while refining those experiences into useful life lessons, fosters success. The refinement of learning to trust again has given me a wonderful wife, my first child, and new perspectives on relationships. My guiding principle to learn, apply, and refine is something I hope my son will use to help guide him as he discovers his own guiding principle.

Even though my feet are still solidly planted on the ground, I'm tackling the sky one star at a time. I hope my story will inspire others to become proactive, and possibly radical, in the pursuit of goals in their own lives.

Robin Dahms

Robin Dahms is the brains and hard work behind Events of Significance, a company dedicated to helping businesses, individuals and organizations create exceptional events. With more than 3 decades of event management experience, Robin takes care of all of the details—from planning and coaching to marketing and logistics. Because different clients have different goals, Robin takes the time to truly understand the intentions of those she works with. Always energetic and driven to help other succeed, she acts as a guide encouraging out-of-the-box thinking and best practices. Her company also offers coaching and training to help presenters make the best impression possible and maximize profits through events and speaking engagements.

Learn more about Robin:
Website: http://www.eventsofsignificance.com/
Social Media Links:
Facebook: Personal: https://www.facebook.com/robin.m.dahms
Facebook: Events of Significance www.facebook.com/EventsOfSignificance?pnref=lhc
LinkedIn: www.linkedin.com/pub/robin-dahms/3a/237/3ab/en
Instagram: https://instagram.com/events_of_significance/
Twitter: @EventsofS

Chapter 10

PURPOSE-DRIVEN LIFE THROUGH SERVANT LEADERSHIP

By Robin M. Dahms

I grew up in Arkansas, which is something I don't tell everyone. People from Arkansas are supposed to be dumber than most and inbred, right? We lived at the top of a hill, a very high hill, in a very large home. Our home overlooked the Country Club Golf Course and the entire city in our small town. We had two new cars, the only SUV made at the time, a pool with custom cabana, a boat, 2 dogs and multiple cats. I was 8 and my sister was 5. My father was a regional director, traveling salesman, and he was very good at sales. His income allowed my mother to stay and home and our family to have all the nice things.

That was not enough for my mother. Her eyes began to wander during my father's frequent out of town trips. She must have been lonely and tired taking on the responsibilities of 2 young children by herself. I understand that now that I am a mom of two active kids! The day-to-day tasks of a home, yard, pool, animals and two small children had to have been exhausting for one person. There must have been very little reward not having your adult partner home to share in the responsibilities, memories or lifestyle. Traveling and bringing home the money had to have been easier than being engaged at home. She had an affair with a prominent attorney in our small town and that was the demise of our family unit. My mom confided in me later in life saying my father was 'unemotionally detached'. I will not be able to confirm in this short chapter all the reasons why I agree with her now. You will have to read my next book titled *Live Differently - Ignite Your Life's Passion*.

The divorce led to a split in everything...family unit, home, cars, money, animals, debt. My mother, sister and I moved into a rental home at the *bottom* of the hill where we used to look down at the 'other people'. Now *we* were the 'other people'. Our home was small and did not have air conditioning. Life as we knew it had completely changed.

The prominent attorney, who later became the prosecuting attorney for the county, was significantly younger than my mother, and I suppose lots of fun for her. He told her from the beginning that he did not like children. She ended up marrying him anyway, and we were able to purchase a home again. The home was a beautiful, average sized home in a safe neighborhood. But life was not kind in that beautiful home, and our family was never safe living there. My step-father was not very kind and cruel to me. We had locked doors in our home that we were not allowed to enter for fear of punishment. I have since found out through counseling that he has *narcissist* personality disorder. Unfortunately, my mom had a *submissive* personality, and she would not prevent him from his outbursts and that eventually was taken out on me. He never physically attacked my sister or mom. I think I was the one he went after because I had a 'smart mouth', and he would not have the disrespect in his home. I did not view him as my authority figure, nor were his actions and behavior worthy of respect. If you know anything about narcissist personality, they will take out anyone (to the death) that does not respect them and hold them in a 'Godlike' stature.

After years of cruel treatment and always being told I was stupid and would never amount to anything and that no one would ever love me, I begged my dad to ask the courts if I could come live with him at the age of 14. The stars aligned and I was on my way to Little Rock, about 30 miles south of the small town where my sister, mother and step-father were to stay. My father and new step-mother had expectations that I had to agree to before coming to live with them. One was that I would attend Mount St. Mary's Catholic Girls School, and I would work onsite after school in the bookstore to help pay for the tuition. I was desperate to get out of my situation and agreed. This was the best decision I had made up until this point and there was hope in this decision. At St. Mary's, I was surrounded by Christian people; I was forced to attend Religion class daily, chapel twice a week, and Mass once a month. It is where I began to feel God's presence through the reading of His daily word.

I had a lot of healing to do; I was not the best person, and I needed help to begin the healing process. I was the St. Mary bully on campus. I was jealous of most of the girls there and did not fit in. There were a lot of wealthy families whose children attended, including a Rockefeller, whose bodyguard accompanied her everywhere except inside the girl's restroom! You would have thought I would have been completely comfortable in that environment considering we grew up with money, but my emotional state was unstable and I was not being nurtured to heal through professional counseling. I ended up getting into a group of Motley Crue/Led Zeppelin bullies wearing parachute pants, chains and a mullet hair cut! We harassed the 'little rich girls' outside of school hours to the point that the police were involved and our parents had to talk with the police and the 'potential victim's' parents to have a serious discussion. These are moments I am not proud of.

My dad got laid off and we could no longer afford our home (again). He later found gainful employment in Houston, TX. He moved to Houston to start the job and find us a proper home. This took longer than expected because we were not able to sell our Little Rock home quickly. Our money was tied up in that home, and we were unable to purchase a new Houston home. My step-mother grew impatient and divorced my father. She sent me to live with my dad in Houston. He lived in one of the poorest apartment complexes because there was no money, but located in a *great* school district.

I felt so relieved and thankful. I was able to 'start-over'. I made an attempt to no longer be that person I used to be. There were temptations in Arkansas, that even at the time, I knew, were not who I wanted to be. I wanted to be more virtuous and good. With this move, God was entering into my life. The first days of 11th grade having no friends, a few girls asked me to sit at their lunch table with them. I was sure they recognized I was eating alone. They were Christian girls who loved God and showed that love to me. They held a 7:00am Christian Bible Study before school each day. They invited me to join them! They invited me to Second Baptist Church for a Christian Concert. It was at that concert that I was brought to tears feeling the Holy Spirit dancing in that auditorium and dancing over my heart! I never told them about my past or how 'bad' I was. This was my chance to begin again as the person I (or God, probably) really me wanted to be.

I made the decision to get my education and live a quality, God-Filled life. My heart changed, and I changed. I had now experienced what it means to 'be new in Christ.'

2 Corinthians 5:17:

Therefore, if anyone is in Christ, his new creation has come: The old has gone, the new is here!

The life lessons I've learned that I want to share:

> Decide fully and commit
> Make the decision and don't look back

Complete the steps necessary to accomplish the goal
Follow through and finish well
Relationships and People are more important that money
Actively seek God's will for your life
Stay clear and love others more than yourself
Create and Expect a Purpose-Driven Life through Servant Leadership

1 Peter 1:2:

…who have been chosen according to the foreknowledge of God the Father, through the sanctifying work of the Spirit, to be obedient to Jesus Christ and sprinkled with his blood: Grace and peace be yours in abundance?

Today, I love people more than anything else in this world. I strive to maintain a servant leadership ministry in all areas of my life and within my team. Jesus is a perfect example of loving others despite their sin.

Mark 2:15:

While Jesus was having dinner at Levi's house, many tax collectors and sinners were eating with him and his disciples, for there were many who followed him.

Anyone that knows me now cannot believe my story. They cannot believe I used to be the feared bully or that I wore parachute pants and listened to AC/DC! I am proud that they cannot believe my story! I am so happy that God loved me enough to get me out of myself and into what HE created me to be.

2 Peter 10: Confirming One's Calling and Election

Therefore, my brothers and sisters, make every effort to confirm your calling and election. For if you do these things, you will never stumble, and you will receive a rich welcome into the eternal kingdom of our Lord and Savior Jesus Christ.

Today my company, Events of Significance, is designed to give others an outlet to share their message from the stage, their message of "Significant Events". We all have a story to tell. Does your story have impact to help a fellow brother or sister? Does it have enough strength to positively change the lives of one or maybe a 1,000 other people? Events of Significance was born of God's design to give others a platform to showcase significance in the world…abundance, purpose, light and hope. God has been gracious to align me with similar people who believe in making a positive difference in other's lives and in our communities.

Zig Ziglar says, "If you help enough people get what they want, you will get what you want."

You were created for great things. What is your purpose? If you need help praying about that, I would love to talk with you. If you *know* what your purpose is and you want to share it with the world, I'd love to invite you to my stage.

God Bless You. Keep looking forward.

Philippians 4:13

I can do all things through Christ who strengthens me.

Sandy Lawrence

Sandy Lawrence is a "people person" who works passionately to take her client's message to the world and help them Break through, Get noticed, and Be known. Her PR skills are available to anyone who needs a truly perceptive Public Relations expert.

Sandy is a publicist, speaker, and creator of DIY PR programs. She is the Founder and CEO of Perceptive Public Relations. She has received awards for being #17 in Houston's Top Social Media Influencers. Sandy is the author of several books, including the *Do It Yourself PR Guide* and *Soar 2 Success in Marketing: 58 Tips to Getting the Word out and Growing your Business*. Sandy's story, *"From Sandra to Sandy and beyond"* was one of the chapters in the first *Share Your Message with the World*.

Learn more about Sandy:

Website: www.perceptivepublicrealtions.com
Email: Sandy@perceptivepublicrelations.com
Social Media Links:
Facebook: www.facebook.com/thesandylawrence
LinkedIn: www.linkedin.com/in/thesandylawrence
Twitter: www.twitter.com/sandylawrence

Chapter 11

THE STORY CONTINUES... WORDS FOR THE JOURNEY

By Sandy Lawrence

I am not sure when I first realized the importance of words. All I know is that a few years ago I started paying attention to particular words and their effect on my life and me. Some words, either in my devotions, a song, or a conversation would just stand out.

I remember when I first heard the words, "know, like, and trust." The importance of those three words, not only in my business life, but also in my spiritual life was astounding. I read from Bob Burg in his book, Go-Giver, "all things being equal, people buy from those they know, like and trust," and I realized that those three words also told the story of my relationship with God, as I continued my journey with Him.

I began to notice other words as they appeared to me when I was reading, praying or meditating, and I started to examine them and look at how they showed up in my life. Without realizing it, I was hearing from God the word or message that He gave me for that moment in my life.

The first word that I "received" a few years ago was the word "believe." I questioned whether or not I really believed. I claimed to the world that I believed God and His word, but did I really? If I did, why this feeling of angst in my heart every time I told someone that I believed. I decided to be completely honest with myself. After all, God could see through any pretense and knew who I was. For an entire year, I took on the word believe. I meditated. I prayed. I declared, and at the end of the year, I realized that I really did believe, without that little feeling (or question) in my heart.

What was next? I began to explore and to journal about a word or words that would show up for me. As I began this year, 2015, I began to look for words that meant something to me. What did they mean?

I invite you to join me now for the rest of this chapter to see where my journey of words took me. These are just a few of the words that I have found and my thoughts about them.

Perspective – A Key Word For My Life

Perspective is looking at the bigger picture of where we are going and taking our eyes off of the day-to-day routine. I was reading a year-long devotion by Rick Warren at the time that I saw this word and was getting a lot of really cool stuff out of it. Following this structure for my devotions gave me perspective.

Another word, integrity, comes to mind. Can I really say to the world that I have integrity? What does integrity mean? I want to tack perfection onto integrity and to be 100 percent honest 100 percent of the time. Is that integrity? Another word that goes with integrity is "authentic," which tells me that I am not perfect. I am not completely honest all the time. Sometimes, to be honest, I am not 100 percent forthcoming on where I am with a project, with my doctor on whether or not I am following her suggestions, or even my nutritionist when following her plan for my healthy life style.

Who does it hurt? Not the doctor, not the client, not anyone to whom I am not being completely honest. It hurts me. It results in my feeling guilty, questioning myself, and writing journals. It hurts my relationship with God and makes me stay away from Him.

I definitely had not planned to write about this topic, it was all about perspective, remember? So how do the two topics relate, or do they? Everything relates in one way or another. I am simply following my thought process here (dangerous as that might be) and will see where it takes us.

My intention is to be open through this process of words to see where God might take me, to listen to His voice and to hear what He is telling me. Is He telling me to look at my perspective about integrity? I think maybe that's it.

So, here are my thoughts. I strive for complete integrity, being honest and straightforward 100% of the time. Looking at that goal from a realistic perspective, I may not reach that until I have a perfect body and mind. So, for now, my goal is to believe that God will love me even when I am not perfect, trust that He will continue to lead my life in such a way as to grow, not only in my relationship with Him, but also in my relationship with others, with my life.

Thank you God for this unexpected message. I believe you. I am learning to trust you and that is helping me to grow in my life here on earth.

Confidence and Approval – Two Words for Today

Are these words related at all? Probably not on the norm. They came to me in my reading and devotions again.

First – confidence! I long for the day when I can say with confidence that I have complete trust in God. I trust His plan for my life. I have confidence that His plan is the best for my life.

Approval. I struggle with wanting approval from family, friends, clients, and even God. When I do not have approval, or even think that I don't, I am unhappy, a little sad, anxious, even frustrated. Why am I so obsessed with approval? It means I have to look good, act good, be good…be perfect in other words. It makes me unhappy to know that someone, anyone, is unhappy with me. How do I get past that?

My prayer is that I learn to trust with confidence and not "worry" about approval from anyone except God. Is that possible? I want my writings to be real, authentic and from my heart. I want people to get to know me, really know me.

Help me to share myself with you. Are these really my thoughts that I am writing or am I saying what I think someone wants me to say. Am I looking for approval even here? That is something for me to examine.

Follow – Commitment – Not Necessarily In That Order!

I love the devotion with Rick Warren and some of the insight from his 365-day devotion guide. Also, I love listening to podcast with Michael Hyatt! And I like my daily dose of Darren Hardy. I learn so much from these great spiritual leaders.

Each day, when I take the time, I get new insights, new thoughts and new words.

Today, it occurred to me, as I am reading about asking for daily provision, that I sometimes, in fact most of the time, take the daily stuff for granted. I don't think about following daily, or about asking for my regular day-to-day needs to be met in my personal or business life.

So, today I prayed for my bills to be paid. I prayed for food, for daily stuff, and I prayed for my business, for the right people, for the right clients and the people to help me take the best care of my clients. I also remembered to be grateful that these needs are met on a regular basis.

What does that have to do with my word for today? I realize that I must follow the insights that I receive, the messages and the desires that come from my Heavenly Father and I desire to commit to him in the day-to-day life that I live. Interesting, that the

Michael Hyatt podcast talked about our schedule, planning it and "following" the plan. Also about being committed to putting the most important things in our schedule first, and then all of the peripheral things will fit in. I once watched a video about big rocks. When we put in the most important things, the big rocks, the little things will all fit in around them.

My biggest rock (other than my devotion time) is exercise time. I always feel like I don't have time. That is one rock I am putting on my schedule!

Contentment and Generosity

What stood out for me today was, first, contentment, "Godliness with contentment is great gain."

I recently completed a three-day mastermind on building my business, being aggressive with sales calls, strategy sessions, and follow up – making money. How do I merge thoughts of aggressively building a profitable business and being content? I struggle with this. For the most part I am content.

Would I love to have more money to do more of the things I enjoy? Absolutely! Does that motivate me to do more? Yes, it does. So how can I be aggressive and content? I will have to think about that.

I am not sure why I am putting these two words together – contentment and generosity. How do contentment and generosity go together? Do they go together? Can I be content and generous? Maybe being generous makes me content.

One of my favorite Bible verses says that we receive based on the same measurement with which we give. So, we give and receive accordingly, and contentment (for me) comes when I am giving. I leave the receiving, and the amount I receive, totally up to God.

To balance this out, I work on my business aggressively, so that I can be more generous with what I give, and in turn, receive according to how I give. I can live with that. This realization gives me a reason for being aggressive in sales and client development.

That to me is how contentment and generosity go together.

Grateful – Today I am grateful

We just finished a rough week. My husband, David, found out he is approved for a transplant, for which I am grateful.

When I first received the news that he was approved I was, at first, grateful and then realized, "Here comes another giant lifestyle change." We have already changed to a plant-based lifestyle and now here we go again. That was my second thought, after my first thought of being grateful.

Life as we now know it will be forever changed and we just got comfortable in this way of living. Uh-oh…I just said a bad word, "Comfortable!" Being comfortable, even though it seems easier, is not where I want to live. All the "fun" and excitement takes place outside the comfort zone, or so "they" say.

Regardless, we are off on another adventure, another leg in this journey called life. I have to admit that writing about it made it seem not so difficult, even adventurous. I will continue to write about it and share, even as I hear of others who are on journeys of their own.

Writing about it puts everything in perspective. Who knew! I guess I have joined the world of writers, journalers and bloggers. Where does this winding road of my life go? It is exciting to find out, as I continue to leave one comfort zone after another. At 71, I am grateful (back to the original word) that I live an exciting, fun, cool life. Thank you God! You know I would never have chosen most of these paths without your gentle (sometimes not so gentle) pushing so I am grateful for you.

Surrender – What Exactly Is Surrender And How Does It Work In Our Lives?

Is there a conflict between being completely surrendered to God and His will for my life and in making a choice and being responsible?

These questions have been showing up for me recently more than in the past.

Note: I want to be completely where God wants me to be in my life. I hear messages about stepping out in faith, moving forward, choosing–and then I hear the surrender word. How can I do both?

I just had surgery this year on my throat, which was a decision or choice that I made. Because of that decision, which was in part to be a healthier person in 2015, I am now limited in what I can do during the healing process. How can I know this was right choice for me to make?

This is rambling, I know. Just putting my thoughts down. No judgment!

Where am I going with this?

I guess I am asking. Is surrender a passive thing? Do I sit back and wait to see what God brings into my life or do I continue to make choices as I see them to make, and then trust in the results or consequences?

God – Just so you know…I am looking for responses from you. Help me to recognize them and not be attached to the outcome.

Is Anything Too Hard For God?

I BELIEVE God can do anything. I believe His word is true.

That's what I tell myself…right? Then, why do I worry about bills that are coming due and little or no money in the bank?

It all comes down to TRUST. Even though I know God is all-powerful, do I really *believe* that He will do for me what He said He would do. Can I trust Him for "little ole me?" Then, it becomes a matter of believing and trusting that *I* matter…at all and to God.

This year my goal is to Pay Attention to Sandy! Learn from the words that play an integral part in this journey called LIFE. So, I am believing and trusting God to help me. There, I said it. I wrote it down and others may see it.

"I trust in the Lord with all my heart. I lean not to my own understanding. In all my ways I acknowledge Him and He directs my path."

Steven Ankerstar

Steven E. Ankerstar is the founder of Afterburner Financial, LLC.—a financial services firm based in Texas. As such, Mr. Ankerstar specializes in private wealth management to provide individuals with a tailored flight plan to achieve their financial goals. Mr. Ankerstar defended this country for 20+ years as an Air Force fighter pilot and now he defends his clients against threats to their financial well-being. Steve speaks regularly on dropping the first bomb of the "Shock and Awe" campaign over Iraq in 2003. Steve can be hired for speaking through his website. Steve's first book is available on Amazon.

Learn more about Steven:

Website: www.afterburner-financial.com
Email: steveankerstar@gmail.com
Phone: (512) 937-6750
Social Media Links:
Facebook: www.facebook.com/afterburnerfinancial
LinkedIn: www.linkedin.com/in/cruiserankerstar

Chapter 12

"THE BEST JOB IN THE WORLD"

By Steven Ankerstar

For the better part of 20 years, I had the best job in the world—serving my country as an Air Force fighter pilot. Even though I am now retired from the military and fully immersed in the next best job in the world, rarely a day goes by without reflecting back on this amazing "call to duty." I came from humble beginnings and like most children I had big dreams, but I lacked a real strategy on how to achieve them. Because of the "shoot for the stars" but still falling short reality of my early years, my peers from my youth were quite shocked when the gangly kid they knew in high school made his mark flying the nation's front-line air superiority fighter of its time—the F–15C Eagle!

I speak regularly to groups on the importance of both *goal setting* and *goal achievement*. The key ingredient to achieving your goals is preparation. And this preparation better be fueled by traits called perseverance and courage. The courage to keep moving forward even when my own mother worried that I might be setting the bar too high and that I would end up in heartbreak. Her reluctance to believe I could achieve such a lofty goal was illustrated on the day that she saw me start the roaring engines to the Eagle and fly it for the first time. She had a look of incredulity that this couldn't be my "little Steve" flying that supersonic jet, but had to be another pilot who replaced me after I taxied down to the of the runway. She still couldn't believe even after seeing it for her own eyes that I was fulfilling my childhood dream of being a fighter pilot.

A few key traits helped me to excel as a fighter pilot. For starters, I love sports, computer games, and math...three ingredients I call my must-haves when I talk to young wannabe fighter pilots. And of course the ultimate "must-have"—unwavering self-confidence. However, I warn aspiring pilots that self-confidence must be honed and not become arrogance; otherwise, it will be a liability. As a fighter pilot, I could not allow my "belief" in my ability to exceed my actual ability or else I could perish (and cause fellow pilots to perish) when making split-second life or death decisions flying beyond the speed of sound. Fortunately, and unbeknownst at the time, I spent most of my youth overcoming this liability, writing checks with my mouth and bravado that I couldn't yet pay. I learned many hard lessons that helped me evolve into a confident, but not overconfident, military leader and fighter pilot.

There were things I knew and believed as a child. I knew I would go to college. I knew I would attempt daunting challenges and believed I would be successful. So, like any child, I bounced from whim to whim—astronaut, firefighter, and engineer— depending on the latest input into my life. That all changed when I saw the movie "Top Gun" during my junior year of high school. After watching this movie, I knew becoming a fighter pilot would be my call to duty.

Several pivotal moments defined my formative pre-fighter pilot times. I worked hard in school, but sometimes got by on my own version of cruise control—I could have worked harder. I had the self-confidence to succeed, but I was not achieving the results I wanted. Something had to change...and that something was me.

The passion was now alive and burning inside after seeing Top Gun and I was convinced this life was for me. I earned a full-ride Air Force ROTC scholarship to Iowa State University. After my sophomore year, I was awarded a slot into navigator training. While this was a highly coveted slot, I was not convinced nor satisfied that being a navigator was my fate. Using the Top Gun reference, "Goose" was the navigator, while "Maverick" was the pilot. To me, it came down to where each person sat in the jet, and I didn't envision myself sitting in back. However, I still had options. I could choose to surrender the navigator slot and compete again for a pilot slot. After much counseling that this path was not wise, I chose this option anyway.

My genius plan backfired. Not only did I not earn a pilot slot, I was also unable to earn my navigator slot back (I had to re-compete for it). Whoops. This was clearly not what I had in mind. Unfortunately, this marked the end of my opportunities to go directly to pilot training after college. My last remaining recourse now was to enter active duty and compete for a pilot training slot. Unfortunately, only a few people get selected out of several hundred highly qualified applicants each year. Not good odds, but odds I could work with— after all, I figured, they did pick a few people.

After three years of service as a maintenance officer, my dream came true—I was selected to attend pilot training. The next step was to earn my wings and finish high enough to earn a fighter. Pilot training was the first time in my life where I had dedicated myself entirely to obtaining my objective. Prior to pilot training, I did what was necessary to excel but hadn't reached my full potential. The results of this enhanced dedication were absolutely amazing and opened my eyes as to what I could accomplish—a truly life-changing discovery!

I finished pilot training as a distinguished graduate and earned a coveted and highly contested spot into the F-15C. Being single at the time, I happily sacrificed my recreational time and enjoyed being what pilot's call "married to my airplane." My pursuit of knowledge and the extra hours per night of studying were rewarded when I developed and honed a commanding level of expertise which set me apart from my peers. Only then did I realize that I skated by "effort-wise" earlier in my life, and I was truly grateful that I had finally discovered what maximum effort and maximum performance was all about. My experience demonstrates what is possible if you have the passion, dedication, and wherewithal to take reaching your goal so seriously that failing becomes inconceivable.

Flying fighters is the best job in the world. The sheer man versus machine aspect of mastering the controls of a multimillion-dollar airplane is the thrill of a lifetime. The roar of the engines as they start up, the vibration in your rib cage from the afterburners kicking in on takeoff, to traveling over the planet at well over the speed of sound are all experiences that words cannot adequately describe. It is an understatement that it takes special people to serve. Dedicating one's life to protecting this country and putting the needs of the country over the needs of their family and themselves is not for everyone. But for the select few, the rewards are enormous—even more so when serving in the cockpit of a lethal war machine. It is beyond an honor.

Flying fighter jets in defense of this country was so amazing that the memories of my experiences while flying will be forever etched in my mind. I had made it. I had done it. I was a fighter pilot. I had slipped the surly bonds of flight and touched the face of God in a $30 million dollar fighter jet. I told a close friend at the time that if I died in my sleep that night, that's okay, my life was complete.

Thankfully, I did not die in my sleep that night, because life for me had just truly begun. Less than two years later, I would be flying F-15Cs in combat over the skies of Iraq during Operation DESERT FOX. That next summer, I flew F-15Cs all over the country as the narrator for the West Coast F-15C Demonstration Team. After three years flying the F-15C, I was selected to fly the F-117 Nighthawk—more commonly known as the stealth fighter.

I was humbled by the opportunities I had while flying the F-117. I quickly became an instructor and spent a large portion of my time flying in "Red Flag" training exercises teaching other combat aviators how to integrate with stealth technology. Also, I flew several airshows around the country including returning home to Ohio to fly an airshow for my parents and friends from high school. However, the joys of these peacetime experiences paled in comparison to the series of events kicked off by 9/11, where I was called upon to do what I had been trained to do—employ combat airpower in defense of this nation.

Everyone knows where they were on 9/11. The only difference for me was that I was combat mission ready in the Air Force's premiere war starting aircraft! The F-117 had launched the opening strikes of Operation DESERT STORM as well as Operation ALLIED FORCE and it was sure to launch the opening strikes of whatever was about to happen. So, while the US was processing the totality of the event, I was in my car going home to pack my bags for an immediate trip to an unknown location for an unknown amount of time. Fear of the unknown did not exist as my body and mind were geared toward making someone pay for the 3,000+ lost lives we will never forget on that fateful day. And I knew I would be on the leading edge of the payback.

As operations over Iraq kicked off, I was honored to have dropped the first bomb of Shock and Awe—the largest continuous single display of airpower the world has ever known—that night from my F-117 stealth fighter on a communications center north of Baghdad. As I approached my first target, I watched hundreds of cruise missiles impact Baghdad just prior to my arrival. I was in "stealth mode" abeam a city that looked like any other city at night. However, the sky lit up with explosions and return fire exactly at the preplanned time of impact. My front row seat for this display was amazing. And then I flew directly over this area minutes later.

When not off at war, other doors were opened for those such as myself who flew fighters. I was very fortunate to fly over Game One of the World Series in 2002 as well as to coordinate flybys for five NFL games and four NASCAR races over the years. Lastly, I was selected as a demonstration pilot finalist for the Air Force Aerial Demonstration Team "Thunderbirds" in 2003 shortly after returning from Operation IRAQI FREEDOM. While I was not selected for the team, the flying tryout portion with the team allowed me to fly closer formation with other aircraft than I ever had before. What an experience!

I concluded the flying portion of my career as commander of pilot training squadron where I mentored students selected for the fighter/bomber track. I often shared my story on what it takes to succeed and I could see the fire start (or continue) to burn in many. I always told my new students that I would trade everything that I have done in the Air Force, just for the opportunity to go back and try to do it all again. That is how amazing the experience was.

You can do the same. Do not be deterred by the thousands of hurdles that stand between you and your passion. I was fortunate to find mine at a young age and then pursue it relentlessly for over a decade prior to achieving it. Every door that closed only meant I had to find more doors to open. My philosophy was (and still is) that it is better to have tried and failed, than to have never tried at all. Whatever your passion is, make it the focal point of your life, work harder than anyone else, and don't let go of your dream.

Dr. Susan M. Quiring

A devastating illness changed Dr. Susan Quiring's career from university professor to owner of a dance and etiquette business, Susan's Ballroom Dance and Class Act Etiquette. A former 4-H agent in Kansas and associate professor at Texas A&M University, Susan holds a doctorate in adult education from Kansas State University. Colleagues and clients describe her as insightful, wise, enthusiastic, and, affectionately, as the "Brazos Valley's Miss Manners." In addition to guest appearances on TV and radio and facilitating study-abroad programs, she helps young and old alike rediscover the power of graciousness and imparts lifelong skills in etiquette and ballroom dance.

Learn more about Susan:

Website: www.SusansBallroomDance.com
Email: susan@susansballroomdance.com
Phone: 979-690-0606
Social Media Links:
Facebook: https://www.facebook.com/pages/Susans-Ballroom-Dance/167741516641862
Facebook: https://www.facebook.com/susan.quiring.1?fref=ts

Chapter 13

GOD, IS THERE A MINISTRY IN DANCE?

By Susan M. Quiring, Ph.D.

Above the heavy beat of "Rock Around the Clock," I heard Veronica giggle and watched her execute a twinkle and a two-way turn. Across the room, her mother beamed at the progress in dance skills her 18-year-old Down syndrome daughter had made. We had already realized that dancing fit Veronica's special needs. "She can't wait for each lesson," her mother wrote. "She is gaining confidence and is becoming more socially accepted." The child, shunned at many events, had friends on the dance floor—especially the guys in my class.

As I shared her mother's happiness, I marveled at how God had orchestrated an abrupt change in my life. He launched me onto an agonizing journey that led away from a busy university career to one I never would've expected.

A Glimpse into My Past

Years spent as a 4-Her growing up and a desire to work with kids led me to a career with the Kansas Cooperative Extension Service. First I was a 4-H agent, later I came to Texas Agricultural Extension Service at Texas A&M University (now Texas A&M AgriLife) as a housing specialist. Through the years, I began to feel I was on a path that wasn't meant for me. An opportunity arose at work to travel to Mexico to live with a family there, and immerse myself in the language, culture, and lifestyle. I jumped at the opportunity, thinking it might be just the change that would redirect me. Seven weeks later I returned home totally immersed alright—with parasites!

A year and a half of intense medical treatments weakened my immune system but not the parasites. No organ in my body functioned properly. Every day was filled with constant pain, a chronic sore throat, dizziness, severe fatigue and brain fog.

One night, unable to sleep, I realized I defined myself by my career with its promotions, great travel, nice paychecks—the world's measures of success. However, I didn't love my job; in fact, when I thought about it, I felt empty, unfulfilled, and directionless. I cried out to God, *"Take the job. Take the retirement benefits. Take the perks. Take all of it. Just bring me peace and a good night's sleep."* For weeks and weeks I had awakened each night, tossing back and forth, fearful of my future. But from that night on, I slept soundly, secure that God was taking care of me.

One day, I lay on the floor with a stethoscope perched on my abdomen, listening to microscopic parasites crawl around inside. (*Isn't that just a pleasant thought?!*) Discouragement overwhelmed me as I languished, weak and in pain. Through that illness and subsequent breakdown of my body—thyroid problems, hormones issues, brain fog, chronic fatigue syndrome, fibromyalgia—my ability to focus became impaired. I found myself too exhausted to move and unable to think. Even bill-paying was taxing.

But I was determined to move forward with God's help. God became my health practitioner. At meals, I'd hold up a forkful of food and ask, *"God, is it all right for me to eat this?"* If I felt any hesitation, I put it down. I turned to alternative medicine. Five months later, the parasites were gone—something I knew only God could accomplish. However, all my other ailments still needed attention. My body had experienced much damage as a result of both the parasites and the continuous medications.

Along with nutritional changes, I started exercising again. I needed some sort of workout, since my illness nearly gave me the brittle bones of osteoporosis. My doctor advised, "Take daily calcium supplements and go to the gym." Knowing I liked to dance, he shared several studies linking health with ballroom dancing. "Dance often," he advised. "It provides a great cardiovascular workout, builds stronger bones, and helps reduce stress."

For two years, I danced for exercise. When tests showed that I'd reversed the bone loss, the doctor said, "Keep beating the pavement to the point you're fatigued, then the next day do more!" Dancing forced me to breathe hard, pumping needed oxygen to my brain. It worked muscle groups and strengthened bone. The fun quotient kicked in the health-enhancing endorphins, and my immune system gradually grew stronger.

While ill, I experienced total dependence upon God as I allowed Him to orchestrate my activities, my diet, and my thoughts. It was my daily seeking the presence of God and His design for my life that brought me through baby steps to start my own business. Despite never having had a business course, God directed me out of my comfort zone and into self-employment.

But how was I going to make a living from a former hobby? I made a list of what I liked to do as an adult and as a child, my skills, my gifts, my core values. I still had a passion for working with children and teens. I wanted to do something that helped people grow in character and confidence. I'd already taught ballroom dancing as a hobby while working at the university. But now I needed more than a hobby. I needed to pay the bills. I realized that I gained much joy and satisfaction from teaching dance, so I started praying, *"God, is there a ministry in dance?"*

Early in my recovery, I attended a Bible conference. I felt like a beat-up rag doll struggling to stay awake. Then the speaker said, "I like to compare my relationship with Jesus Christ to ballroom dancing." I jolted upright. That got my full attention. *"That's it,"* I thought. *"That's how teaching dance is a ministry."* I saw how teaching dance could become my dreamed-for business.

Energized, I felt God flooding my mind with visions of how my relationship with Him is like a dance. A gentleman politely extends an invitation to a lady to join him on the dance floor, where she must follow as he leads. The longer the lady dances with her partner, the more attuned she becomes to his moves and expectations. She knows what position to take, when to hesitate, and when to rise and fall.

"The secret to a beautiful dance consists of one person leading and the other following," I share with my students. "The man's arms and posture create a frame that provides a solid foundation for the lady to feel, to respond to, and to follow. It's like a magical waltz, whether facing backward or forward, whether your steps are quick and purposeful or slow and graceful with a rise and fall."

The couple becomes one body, moving gracefully, effortlessly, responding to gentle cues. A beautiful dance requires surrender, willingness, and attentiveness from one person, and is dependent upon gentle guidance from another. This dance connection is a great formula for marriage, for our Christian walk, for relationships in general. My life "after parasites," healed with the aid of dancing and listening to God, attests to those truths.

Initially my business started slowly, by word of mouth. Others have said, "do what you love, and the money will follow." I am passionate about teaching dance. I genuinely care about people. I love helping people grow with a skill that can last a lifetime.

Another Door Opens

My parents taught me as a young girl to set the table, to be polite, to respect other people and other people's property and possessions. I appreciate what they taught me, and have always thought it important for young people to learn these skills. As an adult, I informally taught etiquette skills to my 4-Hers through table-setting contests and during overseas trips as a counselor with American Institute of Foreign Studies.

But I hadn't considered becoming a certified etiquette coach until two events occurred: first, a woman approached me at the grocery store and asked if I would teach her home school group etiquette; second, the president of a local women's club asked me to teach Cotillion at their venue. I spent the next six months researching, becoming certified, and writing my own programs for kids and a business etiquette course for adults.

Putting It All Together

Through my Brazos Valley Cotillion and summer Class Act Etiquette Camps, which teach both etiquette and dance, I am challenging kids to reach out to others, to be kind, to develop conversation skills. Good character—what we are when no one else is looking—is a natural fit with ballroom dance and etiquette. Through dance skills I watch young men suddenly gain confidence, improve posture, smile, as they realize girls like it that they can dance! I see young girls blossom and recognize their own worth and beauty.

With my adult students, I am continually amazed at God's hand in bringing the right people together, helping mid-life adults enjoy socializing, helping some with major weight loss (one man lost 160 pounds just from dancing), and using my dance classes to keep senior adults active. As I work with businesses and college students on etiquette practices, we realize the quality of our lives depends upon our ability to relate and connect. To build such relationships, we need respect, consideration, and kindness—the heart of my seminars. A simple etiquette lesson can be used as a primer in good morals, ethics, and treatment of others.

Building Character, Confidence and Courtesy has become my mission statement. We are a changing society. A polite society gets along, but a society filled with anger, "busyness," and constant noise is impatient and unkind. Three-fourths of success is people skills. So whether talking about etiquette tools of first impressions, conversation or dining skills, common courtesies, social media etiquette, or dance skills—clients are learning to have respect for others, to value others, to be aware of others' needs. These skills, which are critical in business and social settings, are also fundamental to a Christian life. As William Thourlby has said, *"People, like diamonds, have basic market value, but it is only after they have been polished that the world will pay their real value."*

God, is there a ministry through dance?

Yes, over the years I have learned that, indeed, there is a ministry through dance. My files contain many touching thank-you notes from adult and teenage students, affirming that I have moved into the career that God planned for me. The Divine Dancer gives me purpose in each day as I seek to share the fragrance of Christ and to encourage the beauty and potential in each life I touch. A peek into my files reveals the power of this ministry for young and old alike. One parent appealed to me and said, "Please talk to my suicidal son. You are the only one he will listen to." A 13-year-old girl with social anxiety who asked that I participate in a special program at her school which allows her to meet with me five hours per week to work on both dance and life skills to overcome her anxiety. I minister through dance with couples new as well as tried and true—from preparing wedding couples for their first dance and sharing the analogy of a good marriage represented by the role of lead/follow, to seeing the tears of joy in a woman's eyes as her husband dances with her, satisfying a 30-year longing.

When a parent thanks me for providing good, clean recreation in the community, my heart turns to God in thankfulness. When people seek my counsel outside of dance class for personal problems, I am grateful for the chance to help. When I watch sixty smiling teenagers glide across the room to a beautiful waltz or tango to "Phantom of the Opera," my heart melts.

I believe that C.S. Lewis was speaking to me when he said, "Nothing is really ours until we share it." More doors continue to be open for speaking and sharing one-on-one. I had a great former career in the university setting, but my new profession has given me the desires of my heart (Psalm 20:4).

Vickey Wachtel

An artist who sees the world as a canvas, some paintings are finished, some need to be. Everything is possible with imagination and the faith that it can be done, we just have to dream it to make it so. My desire to be of use has led me to positions with a national insurance firm and an international moving company then to create a retail decorating/remolding business which created the perfect background for my last career choice, real estate. I am the Broker/Owner of Imagine Realty International headquarters in Katy, TX. Today Houston, tomorrow the world.

Learn More About Vickey:

Website: www.ImagineRealtyInternational.com
Social Media Links:
Facebook: www.facebook.com/vickey.wachtel
LinkedIn: www.linkedin.com/in/vickeywachtel
Pinterest: www.pinterest.com/vwachtel/

Chapter 14

"IT STARTED WITH A FEELING"

By Vickey Wachtel

It started with a feeling, no questions were asked, none where needed. It was right and right for a long time then one day it didn't feel right anymore and that should have been the end but I questioned the thought of ending it. More questions came, questions with no answers. If I had ended it before the questions, it would have been easier on everyone concerned without questions, doubts and resentments.

If you have to ask if it's right...chances are...it's not.

How often do you make a decision based on your gut? That feeling that it's right and then feel so gratified that you listened to that inner voice and it worked out just as you hoped or even better than you could have dreamed.

Too often we double think things, question is this the right thing to do and then do not go forward for fear that it might be a mistake and we will feel stupid or foolish if it doesn't work out the way we had planned. Why?

In my life I have found that when I follow my gut it never fails me. Questioning that gut feeling will almost always cause me regret, pain or sorrow.

We have that inner voice for a reason, to guide us through the labyrinth of life, to get to the other side quicker and happier. Some call it a guardian angel, I think there is something to that, at least I like to think that there is someone or something assisting me in the journey, by my side to guide, gently nudge me along when I get side tracked, as I often do.

Recently I was disappointed by someone that I had let in, someone my gut said yes to a couple of years ago. It was a wonderful relationship from the first day and I felt so fortunate that the Universe had sent her to me. I did not ask questions because I knew without a doubt that she was a gift when I needed it. I still feel that way even though that part of my journey has ended.

The phases of our life are a wonder to behold!! I get so excited when I see a new phase start, even though the end of the one before may have been extremely painful at the time, it is inevitable that it come to an end, that is life and understanding life is never a given. Accepting these changes is one of the hardest things we have to do as humans.

Acceptance of changes, not of my doing, in a graceful dignified manner is next to impossible for me. I tend to want to be the one to choose when the relationship is to change or cease to be. That's the "Boss" in me that has been there for as long as I have memory. I have to be the one in control of every situation and this may be a major flaw in my character that after almost 60 years I have not been able to correct. So I have to wonder if it is in need of correcting. I choose to believe we are born with a personality, that it is not created by circumstances or those around us when we are children. The reactions we expose to others may very well be a direct result of what we have gathered along the way, like when a child pitches a fit to get their way and then gets what they wanted...that is a result of circumstances. We do have a choice or should have in how we react to different situations. This has been told to me on so many occasions that it must be true, but if I react as is to be expected or in a trained response and it is not my true nature, is that being honest? I put honesty on the top of the list of things that are of vital importance to me so how do I force a reaction that is not of my honest character? I can't. I truly resent it when I see others not showing their real feelings, I have to ask what are they afraid of? Fear seems to be a driving force in many and I can't relate because fear of showing my true feelings has never been an issue for me.

So having said all that I want the reader to know that I have been accused of being a "Passionate Person" and that means that I feel deeply, express loudly, jump in with both feet and believe that it is my right to control situations that I find myself in to the very best of my ability. I am the "Boss" of my life and if others want to share my space in time for a while they must understand it is on my terms. This is what I choose to believe even though in some cases it's not so.

When the time comes for a relationship to thin or cease we almost always know it in our gut. We start to ask the questions, why did they say that? Why did they do that when they know that is not what I wanted? Why don't they care if I get upset? Why? Why? Why? This is when our gut tells us to end it or limit it in some way, time to pull back not share as much. Time to see it for what it was, a phase, a time of sharing, giving and taking from each other and then to move on. That person needed you for that time and you needed them but the time has come to go your separate ways, to meet new people, to gain more insight and inspiration to carry on. This time can be so painful for some and joyful for others. You may feel guilt for leaving or pushing the other away. This is to be expected and you will find that at these times the one choosing to leave may do things that will upset you, maybe without consciously knowing they are doing it because if they leave and you are upset at them it may ease the pain of them leaving. I have seen it happen over and over. How often have you talked to someone who has lost someone they love and had them tell all things they did wrong while they were together? You may have thought at the time and they very well may have thought it too, that they were simply justifying the departure or trying to get you on their side. Trying hard to protect their feelings of resentment, failure, being made a fool of for trusting that person. They were simply trying to heal and move on.

Loving someone is one of the scariest things we ever have to do as a human. It requires us to be vulnerable, to expose ourselves, leave ourselves wide open for attack and that goes against our natural instinct to protect ourselves. This may be why so many are alone, never fully trusting someone after being hurt once or twice. I find it extremely sad. I too felt that after this last experience of letting someone become so fully enveloped into my life that I would never trust like that again. I said it out loud "I have learned my lesson, I will never let another get so close to me again" having said it and in front of others it must be a true statement. It is not and words spoken in a time of pain may very well have some truth to them but in this case there was very little. I will trust again, I will leave myself wide open for attack because I know that I am here for a reason and I am not the one to question what that reason is. I am the "Boss" of my time and space and others will join, follow, share for a time and then move on and if it makes their departure easier for them to accept by attacking or hurting me then there isn't much I can do about that. I have a huge heart that heals rather quickly when someone else comes in to take their place and they need me for a time, I am thrilled to know that I am here to teach, educate, guide and share this time and space.

I met a gentleman recently and that is not a term that can be used lightly in today's world. What happened to the time when men wanted to be known as a gentleman? I know the universe is always putting people in our lives for a reason and sometimes it only takes a few minutes to get a point across. He volunteers at the Methodist hospital down town driving a golf cart around bringing people to where they are to go and while driving I imagine he talks to most of them because he talked to us without much encouragement. He talked of patience how he works on his own daily and how others would be so much more content if they would work on their own daily. He spoke with such a warm smooth voice that was easily heard over the noise of the busy halls and lobbies of this huge hospital, without much volume at all. It was even easy for my husband to hear, even though he was in the back of the cart, and let's face it he is in need of earing devices now as well. A voice that was so calm and reassuring, and needed at that moment, we were each upset because we do not know down town Houston at all and find it difficult to keep our patience when not knowing for sure if we are in the right building or not and as luck would have it or as the Universe saw to it, we were in the wrong building and having been there wrongly we had the pleasure to meet a lovely lady who also volunteers there to assist people as they get off the elevators. She came here from Louisiana after the hurricane and stayed because she could find work and gives back for the same reason. She was the one who called for the gentleman to take us to the right building. How can we not believe in a power greater than ourselves when the acts and deeds are all around you...when you look for them?

I spent the next 5 hours there waiting for medication to lower my heart rate enough for them to do a 15 minute test, it just would not go down even after 3 pills but after the second injection they got it low enough to do the test, any other time I would have been so upset for this taking so much of my precious time but after spending 2-3 minutes with that wonderful gentleman I was able to lie there and concentrate on lowering my rate without thinking of the time it was taking...that my friends was a miracle pure and simple! Those that know me well know that it is next to impossible for me to not lose it over anything being wasted, much less my precious time

Thank you Universe for all you give and all you take away for all is a treasure to be experienced and enjoyed. Thank you for being my inner voice. Thank you for caring enough to sprinkle my day with miracles and the joy of meeting people at just the right time and right place to make a real difference in my life.

For those of you that choose to leave I thank you as well because by joining me you filled a need I had at that time and by you're leaving I can focus my attention where it is needed next.

William Dick

William "Bill" Dick Jr. holds a Masters degree in Faith Education and Clinical Pastoral Care from The Southern Baptist Theological Seminary, where his diverse philosophies became evident in his personal and professional lives. His progressive and wholly inclusive style and value helped him to find diverse ways to work, live and care deeply and is uniquely qualified to coach, counsel and consult at the intersection of personal, faith, multi-cultural, business and legacy creation. Bill is the founder of the Trans4mation Project and Personal and Executive Coach, HR and Business consultant. Most importantly, Bill's is a proud father of two adult sons, Trey and Sean.

Learn more about William:

Email: billdickjr@trans4mationproject.org
Website: www.trans4mationproject.org

Chapter 15

WHAT TO DO WITH THE REST OF MY LIFE

"A Seven Year Journey"
By William Dick

In 2008 I was working for Hewitt Associates in Orlando, FL when the recession hit. Little did I know that this was just not going to be the end of my dream job and career but going to be the beginning of long seven year journey for me.

I had started with Hewitt Associates as a Project Manager; they were grooming me for the next Unit Manager role that would soon become available. I did what I do best, which is motivate and bring out the best of people. As a former Southern Baptist Minister of 17 years, I met so many personality types and 9 times out of 10 times I could win their heart over to work for the greater good. I used to like to say, "If I can get a group of folks to volunteer their precious personal time for Jesus then I can easily motivate those who are captive and being paid." I joined Hewitt in 1998, I had just moved to Orlando from Clearwater Florida. While at Hewitt I learned the Benefits Outsourcing Call Center business, everything from writing a training and call guide, to answering calls, then to supervising a team of 27.

My almost 11.5 years with Hewitt was filed with recognition for making a difference in people's lives and making a difference in Hewitt's bottom line. I started in the Call Center management roles and finished as an Account Executive managing over 12 million in revenue and some of their most well known Global Brand organizations. When the Orlando Chronicle did an article on diversity I was quoted as saying that "Hewitt was better for me than Church. I felt loved and valuable, I mostly felt that I was called to that Organization to make a difference, and I did. Until 2008 when I was laid off.

Rob, my partner, and I had met in met in Clearwater in 1996 where he owned 2 assisted living facilities, which he sold and moved to Orlando with me so I could take the position with Hewitt. On January 1, 2000 Rob and I put a deposit down on what we thought would be our retirement home in Winter Springs, Florida. It was the perfect home. Rob and I would often sit and dream of our retirement and things we still wanted to do around the house to get ready for that day.

Two Life changing events happened prior to my being laid off from Hewitt in 2008. I was traveling on business to see a client in DC. The meeting was successful and I had planned to spend the night in DC and fly out the next morning to Cincinnati where I was going to visit my Aunt. She had appointed me the executor of her estate and I always tried to visit at least once or twice a year to check on her and her affairs.

While on this trip I also was going to see Rob's mother, Anna. She lives in Silver Springs, MD and we had planned for her to meet me for dinner at my hotel. I love Rob's family as my own, I always will. About an hour before dinner I got a call from my sister, Terry. The phone on the other end was silent. Hearing sobs in the background I spoke firmly, "Terry please tell me what's wrong. Whatever it is we will get through it together just like we did as kids." She muffled out "I HAVE LUNG CANCER". I just kept telling her I loved her and how much having her as my sister meant to me. She was already at stage 4 and the cancer was very aggressive. Later that same day I went down to meet Rob's mother and told her the news about my sister Terry. I liked to refer to Anna as a true eccentric, for her every encounter is a stage. Anna usually made me laugh but we both cried that evening.

As a minister I have had the conversation about illness and even death with hundreds of families over the years, never thinking I would have to have it with my own. When I arrived in Cincinnati to see Aunt Donna I told her that I needed her to help me think through the situation of telling my folks the news of Terry. Deep down I knew Aunt Donna needed as much "Pastoral Care "as my parents. Aunt Donna gave me some good words to remember. "Make sure you tell my folks while they are sitting down and have plenty of water and Kleenex." I said good advice Aunt Donna as I chuckled under my breath. Here is the thing- when you are a minister there is an unspoken expectation that you're stronger than the rest. Fortunately I can put on a good show but truthfully I was a basket case underneath.

I flew back to my home in Winter Springs and couldn't sleep that night. I called my folks when I got in and told them that I wanted to talk to them the next morning and to have some coffee waiting for me. Morning came and I made the 2.5 hour drive to their golf course retirement condo in Hudson, FL. Arriving my Dad had my coffee waiting and I started the conversation with them with, "Well I had a long talk with Terry the other night, she called me while I was traveling and she had something she wanted me to share with both of you." It went as well as you could expect under the circumstances. My sister had Lung Cancer. Of course there was lots of crying and questions. Terry knew I was going to be at Mom and Dads that Day to share the news as she requested. We called her and first my Mom and then my Dad had a time to express their love and hope that she could still beat this.

No one knows why things happen the way they do. But I figured the reason my whole division was being eliminated was because for the next 10 months I drove my parents back and forth to Mississippi from Florida 8 times, which I couldn't have done had I still been working.

After an agonizing, painful treatment, and much slower than what we hoped, there was no further treatment that would make a difference, so Terry entered Hospice. She died in late July. Before passing my sister arranged everything for her funeral.

I spoke at Terry's funeral and my message about her and for us was about Transformation. My sister had raised butterflies on her 5 acres in rural Mississippi with her handpicked and often catalog ordered "butterfly" plants. She would catch them when in season and sell them to brides who wanted to use them during their upcoming wedding. I tell you this to tell you the miracle of that day. Just as I finished telling this story a butterfly landed on the open bible in front of Terry's picture. I didn't see it but I was wondering why everyone was pointing and gasping and crying. I thought I must have been really good to get that kind of a reaction. Come to find out, after everything was over, my brother-in-law's niece had snapped a picture and came up to show me the yellow butterfly that landed perfectly on the Bible at the right time. At that time I gasped and then the tears poured out . . . I just simply said to God "Yes! Thank you for confirming and affirming my sister. All of us gather at your Wonder and the power of Transformations." My sister is at peace and out of pain. She is wherever God is and if there are butterflies in heaven she is one of them.

Jump forward to five years later and I am now at a place that is not unfamiliar but hasn't come as easy as all my other transformations, transitions that I have had to make. I told Rob that I was going to move to Houston to be close to my sons. Both of them were in their early and late 20's and I was ready to be a grandfather. It was one day early in the morning that I felt God's presence while I was walking slowly with our Bichon Frise, Chantel, that I had made this decision. I so much wanted to be a grandfather and I want to be there if and when that time comes. I told Rob I get a job in Houston or we sell the house, whichever comes first is when I move and he was welcome to come with me. He did. By this time we had celebrated 14 years together.

The middle of 2011 my parents and I started to have conversations about them moving closer to me. It was the right thing; the boys and I were the only ones left of the family. Mom came up in February to start looking for an Independent Living Facility. It was only the second facility that my mother saw that she fell in love with. The Conservatory of Champion Forest quickly became their home, in the truest sense as they developed new and lasting friendships.

Every Friday the facility took the residence of The Conservatory for their weekly "errand" day. Mom and Dad both went to go get haircuts at the local home of the $3.99 haircut. Mom and Dad got in the van ready to head back home and the driver decided to take a shortcut over the parking lot curb blockers not realizing that the parking lot on the other side was a 4 foot drop. My mother fell out of her seat because she didn't have her seat belt on. The driver stopped immediately and found my mother wedged between the seat and the door. She was sore and was beginning to bruise badly but she didn't think she needed to be hospitalized. That was December 5th. On New Year's Eve we rushed my mother to hospital. There would turn out to be 6 visits in less than 3 months. She had an infection and there wasn't anything else they could do. Mom died in August of 2013 after a lengthy Hospice stay in a new Nursing and Rehab facility not far from The Conservatory. My world was slowly crumbling. I was exhausted. My get up and go, got up and sat down. I had officially arrived at the point that even I, who had denied so much of my life, couldn't hide this clinical depression.

During this time I lost my job. Up to this point I had done everything in benefits except sell it on the individual, family, and small to mid-size business level, so I decided to get my Life, Health and Accident Insurance License. I then started The Bill Dick Insurance Company, and to be quite honest it floundered. I struggled to find a General Agency and leaders that I could respect. If you didn't know, those in the Insurance industry could be a bunch of "stuffed shirts." That has never been my style and didn't want to start now. My gift has always been my transparency, clinical pastoral style as a coach, leader, consultant, manager and therapist. So you gave up your business? Today I am with an agency led by a gifted and down- to-earth woman whom I trust and have total respect for.

So in the last seven years I lost two jobs, lost my sister and I became self-employed. I lost my mother and I lost my partner and I moved. I also picked up a nasty habit that turned out to be more negative for me than the escape that I hoped it would be. I started seeing a therapist. Let's call her "Diane"; she was a perfect fit for me. I'm a Psych Major and was a Licensed Mental Health Counselor so I had only been on the therapist side of the chair. But Diane has walked my journey with me for two years now and I consider her to be an advisor that has opened me up to embrace new perspectives about life. I grieved terribly for my mother and sister. The dark days and nights that followed manifested in sleeplessness, crying almost hourly and I stopped going to the one place where I found the most help over my life, Church. I talk about my faith everywhere I go. It is such an important part of who I am. At this point I was so tired of crying and I just wanted to get control and be able to attend a service without tearing up.

At the end of March 2015, I was invited to attend a 16-hour webinar over a Saturday and Sunday on the topic of what to do with the rest of my Life. It was being held as a facilitative experiential learning workshop by Sage University. Martin Sage is the Founder and was facilitating this particular course. Sixteen hours of anything is hard to do on a weekend but it turned out to be the right time and right place for me. The process revealed the answer I had been asking for, for seven years, which was, "God what is it exactly I'm being called to do next?" During this time is when the vision of the "The Transformation Project" became a reality.

The rest of the story is still to be written...

Tony Gambone

Tony Gambone is the founder of the Tough Talk Radio Network, founded in 2010. Tony is a professional public speaker with a passion for innovative business practices. His "tough talking" attitude and extensive knowledge of strategic business planning resonate with a wide-ranging group of people. Audiences of all backgrounds can relate to Tony's conversational yet informational speaking style. An accomplished entrepreneur, Tony understands the struggle many start-ups and small businesses face when beginning their business ventures. He not only offers valuable advice; he offers the honest path to success.

Learn more about Tony:

Website: www.TonyGambone.com
Website: www.ToughTalkRadioNetwork.com
Website: www.ToughTalkBusinessNetwork.org
Email: Tony@Tonygambone.com
<u>**Social Media Links:**</u>
Facebook: facebook.com/toughtalkwithtonygambone
Twitter: twitter.com/tonygambone
LinkedIn: linkedin.com/pub/tony-gambone

Chapter 16

AS I CONTINUE TO REINVENT MYSELF

By Tony Gambone

In the first book of *Share Your Message With The World* I wrote a chapter titled *It's Never Too Late to Reinvent Yourself.* I want to continue writing that story in this book because it seems as life moves forward we are always being challenged to either change or reinvent ourselves along the way.

I have to remind myself of this daily. In my first chapter, *It's Never Too Late to Reinvent Yourself,* I explained the journey of having a disabling disease (Crohn's) and how I was given a death sentence at the age of 19. Yes that is correct, I was told that I had only 5 years to live.

I am now blessed to say that 40 years later I truly believe that God has taken Crohn's from me and has allowed me to continue to live without any worry of that disease controlling my life. I know now that God is totally in control of my life and me.

This being said, I want you to know that life is still full of changes and I often wonder what God's new plan for me is. I wake up to a new day every morning but most of the time it is hard not to carry the previous days with me. I want to tell you about my journey of constantly trying to keep up with the changes to improve who I am, what I do and how I can continue to take care of my family.

Please know that I am one of the most blessed people you will ever meet!! But the fact is that I struggle with the day-to-day changes that we are forced to make in life, business and self. When I learned how important it was to build relationships and help others I thought that I had figured it all out. While I do know this to be true, I also know that there is some much more to it.

For instance, I have built a large list of friends and business associates from my relationship building skills. However, there are still many steps that have to happen in life for things to work as planned. I remember in my first chapter of *It's Never Too Late to Reinvent Yourself,* talking about having a plan and then having to re-write that plan. I am still re-writing the plan from time to time. This was becoming frustrating until I recognized that life is full of changes and the only thing that makes sense is to keep up with the ways to improve who we are so that we can be better at being the person we want to be.

Sometimes I don't really think I am sure of who I am supposed to be or what I am supposed to do with this life. I know what I would like to do but that doesn't always seem to be what God has planned for me. So what do I do when things don't go the way I want them to?

I could just try harder for a longer period of time. I could keep reading my Bible and try to figure out what God has planned for me. I could give up what I worked for in my business and get a job. Wow, as I write this I am getting overwhelmed!!!

It not hard to get overwhelmed in today's world, things are moving fast and things are loud and distracting. So what do we do to stay committed to the changes needed in our world? For me, I find that I pray but most of the time I don't hear or see the message God has for me, or is it that I am not wanting to know the answer? I know for sure that it is never easy and probably never will be easy. But I have learned that if I truly give it to God *and* I am willing to do whatever He puts in front of me I will be able to commit to reinventing myself for all the right reasons.

As a husband, father and a business owner I feel the responsibility to be a leader. So as a leader how do you give up control and totally trust God to get you there? I think, for me, the only way I can commit to being the best leader possible is to surrender to God and allow him to be the leader. This does not mean that I have to give up my position as the leader of my family or my business. What it means is that I have to give up the control and just be the leader that God intended me to be.

I know that reading this might make you roll your eyes and wonder if I am for real. Well I sometime roll my eyes and ask myself if I am for real. But what I have to do is look back over my life and recognize that everything that has happened has not been because of me. I can say that I take responsibility for the wrong things that I have done and I like to think that some of the good things are because of me to. But at the end of the day I have only been doing what God has had planned for me even before I was breathing air on earth.

As I compiled over forty authors in the two compilation books I have often said this one statement, "No one cares about what you do until they know who you are." I know that this is true but the one thing I did not realize until just now is that we don't really care about what we ourselves do until we know more about who we really are. Most of us are not willing to tell that story even to ourselves.

I think that a lot of us are stuck on who we want to be and not on who we really are. In order to be whom we want to be we need to know why we are who we are today. We also need to know what we need to change in order to be who we want to be. A lot of the time we will never become who we are supposed to be unless we give up control and surrender to God and let Him be the leader.

I think that we were all born to be leaders. The problem with most of us is that we don't realize that being a leader has nothing to do with being in charge. God allows us to be in charge of our own lives and for me this is when I realized that reinventing myself was a very important part of the puzzle.

As a person have you ever thought about making the changes necessary for you to be a better person? In the beginning of this chapter I talked about building relationships with others. I think it is impossible to build good relationships with others without first improving yourself first.

This is why it is so important to revisit your journey in life. Learn how you have gotten to where you are today. Are you happy where you are today? What can you do to change? How you can reinvent yourself to be the person God intended you to be?

It is probably safe to say that everyone reading this chapter might not trust God as much as I am trying to trust God, but at the end of the day who are you trusting to help you to be the leader you want to be?

As I wrap up this story I would like to assure you that I will continue to reinvent myself through Gods plan and I will keep sharing the Messages with you through Compilation Books. I hope that reading my story will help you to tell your story. It is so important for the people in and around your life to know who you really are and how you became who you are.

If you, like most people, think that something drastic has to happen before you have a story worth telling I want to make sure that you know that God has created us all equal and that all of us have a message to share. Be sure to tell your story today even if you start by telling it to yourself.

We are always looking at where we are or where we want to go but we never look at where we been and how we made it through it. These are the journeys that will allow you to see how Awesome God really is. Remember to start building relationships with people by asking them questions that allow you to learn more about them. Make sure to be authentic about who you really are and not fall into the trap of trying to be who others think you should be.

I wanted to repeat something that was at the end of my first story in Volume I of Share Your Message With The World, which is "Remember, we were all created equal and the only thing that can keep you from succeeding is *you.*" Here is one of the best tips I was given from a friend, "When your why is big enough, your how will show up.

The end for this chapter that I want leave you with is this – *Serve Whole-heartedly as if you were serving the Lord.* Ephesians 6:7

The End

Learn more about Volumes I and II

www.ShareYourMessageWithTheWorld.com

Become an Author in Vol. III
Email: Tony@TonyGambone.com

Printed in the United States
By Bookmasters